Book Insert

Reading Texts

JOST NICKEL'S
FILL BOOK
A SYSTEMATIC & FUN APPROACH TO FILLS

CD INSIDE

67 MP3 FILLS AND 20 VIDEOS ONLINE

Switch & Path Orchestration
Moving Around the Kit
Clockwise & Counterclockwise
Step–Hit–Hi-Hat
Hand & Foot Roll
Cymbal Choke
Stick Shot
Flam Fills
Blushda
Diddle Kick

Alfred

Reading Text 1 (4- and 2-Note Groupings Using Sixteenth Notes)

Two bars in $\frac{4}{4}$ time
Subdivision of the fills: **Sixteenth notes**
Grid of underlying rhythm: **Eighth notes**

1.

4	4	4	4	2 4	4	4	2
1 +	2 +	3 +	4 +	1 +	2 +	3 +	4 +

2.

4	2 4	2 4	2 4	2 4	4
1 +	2 +	3 +	4 +	1 +	2 +	3 +	4 +

3.

2 4	2 4	2 4	2 4	2 4	2
1 +	2 +	3 +	4 +	1 +	2 +	3 +	4 +

4.

4	4	2 4	4	2 4	2 4	2
1 +	2 +	3 +	4 +	1 +	2 +	3 +	4 +

5.

4	4	4	2 4	4	4	2 4
1 +	2 +	3 +	4 +	1 +	2 +	3 +	4 +

6.

4	2 4	4	2 4	4	2 4	2
1 +	2 +	3 +	4 +	1 +	2 +	3 +	4 +

7.

2 4	4	4	2 4	4	2 4	2
1 +	2 +	3 +	4 +	1 +	2 +	3 +	4 +

8.

2 4	2 2 4	2 4	2 4	4	2
1 +	2 +	3 +	4 +	1 +	2 +	3 +	4 +

9.

4	4	2 2 2 4	2 2 4	2 4
1 +	2 +	3 +	4 +	1 +	2 +	3 +	4 +

Reading Text 2 (4- and 3-Note Groupings Using Sixteenth Notes)

Two bars in $\frac{4}{4}$ time
Subdivision of the fills: **Sixteenth notes**
Grid of underlying rhythm: **Sixteenth notes**

1.

4	3	4	3	4	3	4	3	4

1	e	+	a	2	e	+	a	3	e	+	a	4	e	+	a	1	e	+	a	2	e	+	a	3	e	+	a	4	e	+	a

2.

3	4	3	4	3	4	3	4	4

1	e	+	a	2	e	+	a	3	e	+	a	4	e	+	a	1	e	+	a	2	e	+	a	3	e	+	a	4	e	+	a

3.

4	4	3	3	4	4	3	3	4

1	e	+	a	2	e	+	a	3	e	+	a	4	e	+	a	1	e	+	a	2	e	+	a	3	e	+	a	4	e	+	a

4.

3	4	4	3	4	3	3	4	4

1	e	+	a	2	e	+	a	3	e	+	a	4	e	+	a	1	e	+	a	2	e	+	a	3	e	+	a	4	e	+	a

5.

3	4	3	4	4	3	4	4	3

1	e	+	a	2	e	+	a	3	e	+	a	4	e	+	a	1	e	+	a	2	e	+	a	3	e	+	a	4	e	+	a

6.

4	3	4	4	3	4	3	4	3

1	e	+	a	2	e	+	a	3	e	+	a	4	e	+	a	1	e	+	a	2	e	+	a	3	e	+	a	4	e	+	a

7.

4	4	3	4	4	3	4	4	+2

1	e	+	a	2	e	+	a	3	e	+	a	4	e	+	a	1	e	+	a	2	e	+	a	3	e	+	a	4	e	+	a

8.

3	3	3	4	3	4	3	4	3	+2

1	e	+	a	2	e	+	a	3	e	+	a	4	e	+	a	1	e	+	a	2	e	+	a	3	e	+	a	4	e	+	a

Reading Text 3 (4- and 3-Note Groupings Using Eighth-Note Triplets)

Two bars in $\frac{4}{4}$ time
Subdivision of the fills: **Eighth-note triplets**
Grid of underlying rhythm: **Eighth-note triplets**

1.

4		3	4		3	4		3	3	
1	+	a	2	+	a	3	+	a	4	+	a	1	+	a	2	+	a	3	+	a	4	+	a

2.

3 4 3 4 3 4 3

| 1 | + | a | 2 | + | a | 3 | + | a | 4 | + | a | 1 | + | a | 2 | + | a | 3 | + | a | 4 | + | a |

3.

4 4 3 3 4 4 +2

| 1 | + | a | 2 | + | a | 3 | + | a | 4 | + | a | 1 | + | a | 2 | + | a | 3 | + | a | 4 | + | a |

4.

3 4 3 4 4 3 3

| 1 | + | a | 2 | + | a | 3 | + | a | 4 | + | a | 1 | + | a | 2 | + | A | 3 | + | a | 4 | + | a |

5.

3 4 3 3 4 3 4

| 1 | + | a | 2 | + | a | 3 | + | a | 4 | + | a | 1 | + | a | 2 | + | a | 3 | + | a | 4 | + | a |

6.

3 3 4 3 3 4 4

| 1 | + | a | 2 | + | a | 3 | + | a | 4 | + | a | 1 | + | a | 2 | + | a | 3 | + | a | 4 | + | a |

7.

3 4 4 4 3 4 +2

| 1 | + | a | 2 | + | a | 3 | + | a | 4 | + | a | 1 | + | a | 2 | + | a | 3 | + | a | 4 | + | a |

8.

4 3 4 4 3 4 +2

| 1 | + | a | 2 | + | a | 3 | + | a | 4 | + | a | 1 | + | a | 2 | + | a | 3 | + | a | 4 | + | a |

Reading Text 4 (6- and 3-Note Groupings Using Sixteenth-Note Triplets)

Two bars in $\frac{4}{4}$ time
Subdivision of the fills: **Sixteenth-note triplets**
Grid of underlying rhythm: **Eighth notes**

1. 6 6 6 6 3 6 6 3
1 + 2 + 3 + 4 + 1 + 2 + 3 + 4 +

2. 6 3 6 3 6 3 6 3 6 6
1 + 2 + 3 + 4 + 1 + 2 + 3 + 4 +

3. 3 6 3 6 3 6 3 6 3 6 3
1 + 2 + 3 + 4 + 1 + 2 + 3 + 4 +

4. 6 6 3 6 6 3 6 3 6 3
1 + 2 + 3 + 4 + 1 + 2 + 3 + 4 +

5. 6 6 6 3 6 6 6 3 6
1 + 2 + 3 + 4 + 1 + 2 + 3 + 4 +

6. 6 3 6 6 3 6 6 3 6 3
1 + 2 + 3 + 4 + 1 + 2 + 3 + 4 +

7. 3 6 6 6 3 6 6 3 6 3
1 + 2 + 3 + 4 + 1 + 2 + 3 + 4 +

8. 3 6 3 3 6 3 6 3 6 6 3
1 + 2 + 3 + 4 + 1 + 2 + 3 + 4 +

9. 6 6 3 3 3 6 3 3 6 3 6
1 + 2 + 3 + 4 + 1 + 2 + 3 + 4 +

Reading Text 5 (6- and 4-Note Groupings Using Sixteenth-Note Triplets)

Two bars in $\frac{4}{4}$ time
Subdivision of the fills: **Sixteenth-note triplets**
Grid of underlying rhythm: **Eighth-note triplets**

1.

4	4	4	6	6	6	6	4	4	4

| 1 | + | a | 2 | + | a | 3 | + | a | 4 | + | a | 1 | + | a | 2 | + | a | 3 | + | a | 4 | + | a |

2.

| 4 | 6 | 4 | 6 | 4 | 6 | 4 | 6 | 4 | 4 |

| 1 | + | a | 2 | + | a | 3 | + | a | 4 | + | a | 1 | + | a | 2 | + | a | 3 | + | a | 4 | + | a |

3.

| 4 | 4 | 6 | 4 | 4 | 6 | 4 | 4 | 6 | 6 |

| 1 | + | a | 2 | + | a | 3 | + | a | 4 | + | a | 1 | + | a | 2 | + | a | 3 | + | a | 4 | + | a |

4.

| 6 | 4 | 4 | 6 | 6 | 4 | 4 | 6 | 6 | +2 |

| 1 | + | a | 2 | + | a | 3 | + | a | 4 | + | a | 1 | + | a | 2 | + | a | 3 | + | a | 4 | + | a |

5.

| 4 | 6 | 4 | 4 | 6 | 4 | 6 | 6 | 4 | 4 |

| 1 | + | a | 2 | + | a | 3 | + | a | 4 | + | a | 1 | + | a | 2 | + | a | 3 | + | a | 4 | + | a |

6.

| 4 | 4 | 6 | 4 | 6 | 6 | 4 | 6 | 4 | 4 |

| 1 | + | a | 2 | + | a | 3 | + | a | 4 | + | a | 1 | + | a | 2 | + | a | 3 | + | a | 4 | + | a |

7.

| 6 | 4 | 6 | 4 | 4 | 6 | 4 | 6 | 6 | +2 |

| 1 | + | a | 2 | + | a | 3 | + | a | 4 | + | a | 1 | + | a | 2 | + | a | 3 | + | a | 4 | + | a |

8.

| 4 | 6 | 6 | 4 | 6 | 6 | 4 | 6 | 6 |

| 1 | + | a | 2 | + | a | 3 | + | a | 4 | + | a | 1 | + | a | 2 | + | a | 3 | + | a | 4 | + | a |

Reading Text 6 (8- and 4-Note Groupings Using 32nd Notes)

Two bars in $\frac{4}{4}$ time
Subdivision of the fills: **32nd notes**
Grid of underlying rhythm: **Eighth notes**

1.

8		8		8		8		4	8		8		8		4
1	+	2	+	3	+	4	+	1	+	2	+	3	+	4	+

2.

8		4	8		4	8		4	8		4	8		8	
1	+	2	+	3	+	4	+	1	+	2	+	3	+	4	+

3.

4	8		4	8		4	8		4	8		4	8		4
1	+	2	+	3	+	4	+	1	+	2	+	3	+	4	+

4.

8		8		4	8		8		4	8		4	8		4
1	+	2	+	3	+	4	+	1	+	2	+	3	+	4	+

5.

8		8		8		4	8		8		8		4	8	
1	+	2	+	3	+	4	+	1	+	2	+	3	+	4	+

6.

8		4	8		8		4	8		8		4	8		4
1	+	2	+	3	+	4	+	1	+	2	+	3	+	4	+

7.

4	8		8		8		4	8		8		4	8		4
1	+	2	+	3	+	4	+	1	+	2	+	3	+	4	+

8.

4	8		4	4	8		4	8		4	8		8		4
1	+	2	+	3	+	4	+	1	+	2	+	3	+	4	+

9.

8		8		4	4	4	8		4	4	8		4	8	
1	+	2	+	3	+	4	+	1	+	2	+	3	+	4	+

Reading Text 7 (6- and 4-Note Groupings Using 32nd Notes)

Two bars in $\frac{4}{4}$ time

Subdivision of the fills: **32nd notes**

Grid of underlying rhythm: **Sixteenth notes**

1.

6	6	6	6	6	6	6	6	6	6	+4

1 e + a 2 e + a 3 e + a 4 e + a 1 e + a 2 e + a 3 e + a 4 e + a

2.

| 6 | 4 | 6 | 4 | 6 | 4 | 6 | 4 | 6 | 4 | 6 | 4 | +4 |

1 e + a 2 e + a 3 e + a 4 e + a 1 e + a 2 e + a 3 e + a 4 e + a

3.

| 4 | 6 | 4 | 6 | 4 | 6 | 4 | 6 | 4 | 6 | 4 | 6 | +4 |

1 e + a 2 e + a 3 e + a 4 e + a 1 e + a 2 e + a 3 e + a 4 e + a

4.

| 6 | 4 | 6 | 6 | 4 | 4 | 6 | 6 | 4 | 6 | 6 | 4 | +2 |

1 e + a 2 e + a 3 e + a 4 e + a 1 e + a 2 e + a 3 e + a 4 e + a

5.

| 4 | 6 | 4 | 6 | 6 | 4 | 4 | 6 | 4 | 6 | 6 | 6 | +2 |

1 e + a 2 e + a 3 e + a 4 e + a 1 e + a 2 e + a 3 e + a 4 e + a

6.

| 4 | 6 | 6 | 4 | 6 | 4 | 4 | 6 | 4 | 6 | 6 | 4 | 4 |

1 e + a 2 e + a 3 e + a 4 e + a 1 e + a 2 e + a 3 e + a 4 e + a

7.

| 6 | 6 | 6 | 4 | 4 | 6 | 6 | 4 | 4 | 6 | 4 | 4 |

1 e + a 2 e + a 3 e + a 4 e + a 1 e + a 2 e + a 3 e + a 4 e + a

8.

| 6 | 4 | 4 | 6 | 4 | 6 | 6 | 4 | 6 | 4 | 4 | 6 | 4 |

1 e + a 2 e + a 3 e + a 4 e + a 1 e + a 2 e + a 3 e + a 4 e + a

9.

| 6 | 6 | 4 | 4 | 6 | 6 | 4 | 4 | 6 | 6 | 4 | 6 | +2 |

1 e + a 2 e + a 3 e + a 4 e + a 1 e + a 2 e + a 3 e + a 4 e + a

Reading Text 8 (3-, 5-, and 7-Note Groupings Using Sixteenth Notes I)

Two bars in $\frac{4}{4}$ time
Subdivision of the fills: **Sixteenth notes**
Grid of underlying rhythm: **Sixteenth notes**

3- and 5-note groupings

1.

2.
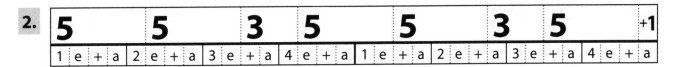

3.
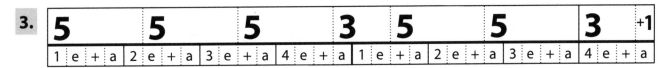

3- and 7-note groupings

4.

5.

| 3 | 3 | 7 | | 3 | 3 | 7 | | | 3 | 3 | |

6.

| 7 | | 7 | | 3 | 7 | | 3 | 3 | +2 |

5- and 7-note groupings

7.

| 5 | 7 | | 5 | 7 | | 7 | +1 |

8.

| 7 | 5 | 7 | | 7 | 5 | +1 |

9.

| 5 | 5 | 7 | | 5 | 5 | 5 |

Reading Text 9 (3-, 5-, and 7-Note Groupings Using Sixteenth Notes II)

Two bars in $\frac{4}{4}$ time

Subdivision of the fills: **Sixteenth notes**

Grid of underlying rhythm: **Sixteenth notes**

1.

3	3	5	5	7	7	+2
1 e + a 2 e + a 3 e + a 4 e + a	1 e + a 2 e + a 3 e + a 4 e + a

2.

5	3	7	7	3	5	+2
1 e + a 2 e + a 3 e + a 4 e + a	1 e + a 2 e + a 3 e + a 4 e + a

3.

7	7	3	5	3	5	+2
1 e + a 2 e + a 3 e + a 4 e + a	1 e + a 2 e + a 3 e + a 4 e + a

4.

5	3	3	7	7	5	+2
1 e + a 2 e + a 3 e + a 4 e + a	1 e + a 2 e + a 3 e + a 4 e + a

5.

5	3	7	3	7	7
1 e + a 2 e + a 3 e + a 4 e + a	1 e + a 2 e + a 3 e + a 4 e + a

6.

7	3	3	3	3	5	3	5
1 e + a 2 e + a 3 e + a 4 e + a	1 e + a 2 e + a 3 e + a 4 e + a

7.

3	7	7	5	3	3	3	+1
1 e + a 2 e + a 3 e + a 4 e + a	1 e + a 2 e + a 3 e + a 4 e + a

8.

3	7	5	3	7	3	3	+1
1 e + a 2 e + a 3 e + a 4 e + a	1 e + a 2 e + a 3 e + a 4 e + a

9.

3	3	3	5	5	7	5	+1
1 e + a 2 e + a 3 e + a 4 e + a	1 e + a 2 e + a 3 e + a 4 e + a

Reading Text 10 (3-, 5-, and 7-Note Groupings Using Eighth-Note Triplets I)

Two bars in $\frac{4}{4}$ time
Subdivision of the fills: **Eighth-note triplets**
Grid of underlying rhythm: **Eighth-note triplets**

3- and 5-note groupings

1.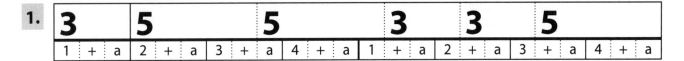

2.

3.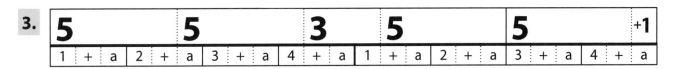

3- and 7-note groupings

4.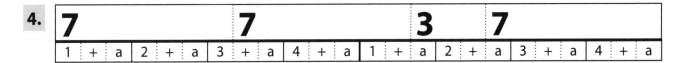

5.

6.

5- and 7-note groupings

7.

8.

9.

Reading Text 11 (3-, 5-, and 7-Note Groupings Using Eighth-Note Triplets II)

Two bars in $\frac{4}{4}$ time

Subdivision of the fills: **Eighth-note triplets**

Grid of underlying rhythm: **Eighth-note triplets**

1.

3	3	5		5		7			+1

| 1 | + | a | 2 | + | a | 3 | + | a | 4 | + | a | 1 | + | a | 2 | + | a | 3 | + | a | 4 | + | a |

2.

7			3	3	5		5		+1

| 1 | + | a | 2 | + | a | 3 | + | a | 4 | + | a | 1 | + | a | 2 | + | a | 3 | + | a | 4 | + | a |

3.

5		5		3	7			3		+1

| 1 | + | a | 2 | + | d | 3 | + | a | 4 | + | a | 1 | + | a | 2 | + | a | 3 | + | a | 4 | + | a |

4.

3	7			7			5		+2

| 1 | + | a | 2 | + | a | 3 | + | a | 4 | + | a | 1 | + | a | 2 | + | a | 3 | + | a | 4 | + | a |

5.

7			3	5		7			+2

| 1 | + | a | 2 | + | a | 3 | + | a | 4 | + | a | 1 | + | a | 2 | + | a | 3 | + | a | 4 | + | a |

6.

5		3	7			7			+2

| 1 | + | a | 2 | + | a | 3 | + | a | 4 | + | a | 1 | + | a | 2 | + | a | 3 | + | a | 4 | + | a |

7.

7			3	3	3	5		3	

| 1 | + | a | 2 | + | a | 3 | + | a | 4 | + | a | 1 | + | a | 2 | + | a | 3 | + | a | 4 | + | a |

8.

5		3	3	7		3	3	

| 1 | + | a | 2 | + | a | 3 | + | a | 4 | + | a | 1 | + | a | 2 | + | a | 3 | + | a | 4 | + | a |

9.

3	7			3	3	5		3	

| 1 | + | a | 2 | + | a | 3 | + | a | 4 | + | a | 1 | + | a | 2 | + | a | 3 | + | a | 4 | + | a |

Thanks

My special thanks go to:

Harald Wester for his great advice, precise work, and endurance

Sonor Drums: Thomas Barth and Karl-Heinz Menzel

Meinl Cymbals & Percussion: Norbert Saemann, Chris Brewer, and Stephan Hänisch

Vic Firth Sticks: Joe Testa and Frank Rohe (M&T)

Remo Drumheads: Chris Hart, Gary Mann, and Nico Nevermann (Gewa)

Ahead Armor Cases: Curt Doernberg (Musik Wein)

Beyerdynamic Microphones: Bernd Neubauer

I dedicate this book to my wife, **Mareike**, and to my daughters, Alma and Mathilde.

www.jostnickel.com

Advice

The attached CD contains MP3 files that can be used with any MP3-compatible hardware such as computers, tablets, MP3 players, most CD players, and most car stereos. Once copied onto your computer, these sound files can be imported into any MP3 player, such as an iPod.

Note: Some older model CD players and car stereos may not be able to read the enclosed MP3 data disc. If this is the case, you have permission to save these files onto your computer and use a program such as iTunes to burn new audio CDs, which will be playable on your current CD player. Incorrect handling may cause the damage of an incompatible device. In these cases, the manufacturer's liability is excluded.

Alfred Music
LEARN • TEACH • PLAY

© 2017 by **Alfred** Music Publishing GmbH
info@alfredverlag.de
alfredverlag.de | alfredmusic.de
alfred.com | alfredUK.com

Cover Design: Gerhard Kühne
Engraving: Jost Nickel
Editors: Thomas Petzold & Raj Mallikarjuna
English translation: Gemma Hill
Item #: 20256US (book & CD)
ISBN-10: 3-943638-35-9
ISBN-13: 978-3-943638-35-6

CD Recording: Jost Nickel
Mix: Jost Nickel
Cover photo by Gerhard Kühne
Photo on page 3 © Inga Seevers
Photos on pages 11, 16, and 46 © Marco Hammer
Photos on pages 11 and 44 © Elle Jaye
Photos on pages 17–20, 43, 102, 113 by Jost Nickel
Photos on pages 23 and 141 © Drumeo
Photo on page 35 © Mario Schmitt
Photo on page 60 © Arnd Geise
Photo on page 142 © Mareike Nickel
Photo on page 142 © Ingo Baron

Jost Nickel's FILL BOOK

Preface

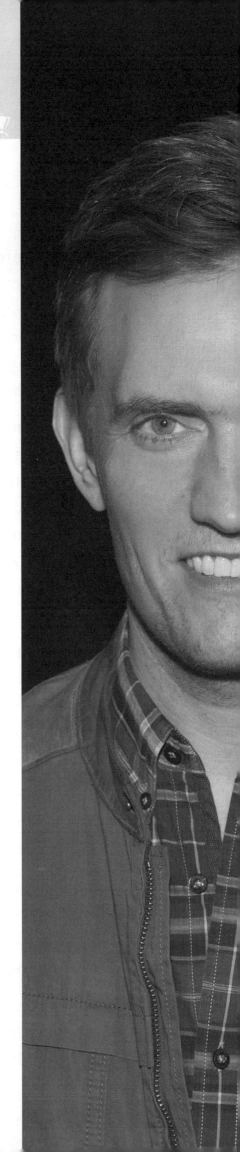

I remember clearly how, ten minutes before my audition with **Jan Delay & Disko No.1**, I sat in front of the practice room in my car and briefly collected my thoughts. It was obvious it would only come down to how the songs grooved with me on the drums. I focused on the right tempo, groove, and playing together with the band, and I deliberately decided to just play simple fills.

Why only simple fills? To be blunt, I wanted to avoid the impression that I needed to prove my ability to play complicated fills, and I didn't want the music to suffer from too many, or inappropriately placed, fills.

After Jan had chosen me, I started to reach deeper into my box of tricks for fills. On the one hand, it makes the music more enjoyable and, on the other, it is simply great fun.

Fun is the key word. I simply enjoy dealing with the instrument and especially with fills.

Whether I play these fills within a band context depends completely on the music and the circumstances. If I have a certain idea for a fill (or a groove) when I'm practicing, I don't consciously think about whether it is usable (or seems usable). If it's fun to play, then it's good.

This book should be fun and helpful so you can understand the basic theory of the respective fills and can get to a place where you can invent your own. I believe all rhythmic concepts in this book (*Chapters 1 to 6*) are current and important because they can be used universally. Some of the orchestration ideas in the last part of the book (*Chapters 7 to 12*) are quite unique, as I incorporate ideas I personally like to use in fills and solos.

As with everything else when it comes to learning the drums, decide on what and when you play according to your taste.

Jost Nickel

P.S. You can find **online video examples** at my website **www.jostnickel.com**.

Contents

Contents

Book Insert: Reading-Text Exercises

How to Work with This Book

Subdivision of Fills and Subdivision of the Underlying Rhythms

With fills, the subdivision you choose is crucial. This obviously depends mostly on the tempo: at a tempo of 60 it is easier to play fills using 32nd notes than it would be at 120.

If you would like to play a very fast fill at 120, you would probably choose a subdivision of sixteenth-note triplets. When you urgently need to play a very fast fill at 80, you may choose 32nd notes instead.

The sophistication of a fill doesn't just depend on the subdivision. The difficulty of fills is essentially determined by the underlying rhythm. You can play your fill using sixteenth notes (or any other subdivision) with either a simple or a more complicated underlying rhythm. In fact, the simpler the underlying rhythm is, the simpler you can keep the fills in perspective, which is indispensable. Even with fills that use sixteenth-note triplets and 32nd notes, the underlying rhythm is often much simpler (often in eighth notes) than the tempo the fill suggests.

Being Aware of the Underlying Rhythm

You should always be aware of the underlying rhythms. They will always be, where necessary, below the fills in the notated examples of this book as a guide.

Here are two ways in which to understand the underlying rhythm taken from *Example 1* in *Chapter 1* (*page 12*). In this fill, both the subdivision of the fill and the subdivision of the underlying rhythm utilize sixteenth notes. First, here is *Example 1* from *Chapter 1* with the underlying rhythm in *line 2*:

Example 1 (3-note grouping over a bar with the underlying rhythm in line 2)

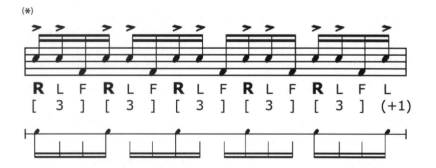

R = right hand
L = left hand
F = foot

This is how to make the underlying rhythm clear:

1. Play the fill in bar 1, and in bar 2, play the rhythm on the snare drum. Just play alternating sixteenth notes on the snare drum, and stress the rhythm. At the same time, you can play the quarter-note pulse on the hi-hat (foot) to enhance your understanding even further.

(*) *Because all the notated examples in this book are in $\frac{4}{4}$ time, time signatures have been omitted.*

Example 1.1 (Rhythm on the snare drum)

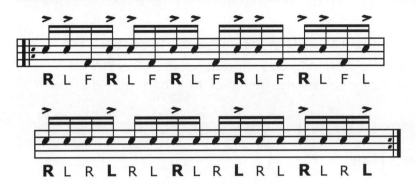

2. Play the fill in bar 1, and in bar 2, play a groove with the underlying rhythm as a bass-drum figure:

Example 1.2 (Groove with rhythm in the bass drum)

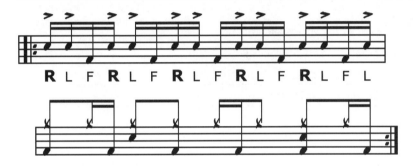

Practice? Practice!

In my opinion, there are three distinctive phases to practicing fills:

Phase 1: Introductory Phase

Because you are dealing with something completely new, first, sort out the hands (and feet) so you get to know the movements. This phase is relatively short. After a while you don't need to think about which hand plays which instrument.

Tip

Take *5 to 10 minutes* per practice session to get to know what you are playing. Familiarize yourself with the movements of one fill by playing it several times in a row without a definite tempo. It may be helpful to speed up or slow down while playing the fill.

Phase 2: Endurance Phase

The new fill is now familiar, and sticking and orchestration are sorted out. Now it's time to play the fill fluidly, to keep an overview of the pulse, to always play at a solid tempo, to play the fill in combination with a groove, to pay attention to a good sound, and to increase the tempo. This phase takes the longest.

It will be helpful to have a concrete idea of how long you'd like to work on each respective exercise per day. In this book, you'll find out how to practice, which I'll go into in more detail.

Phase 3: Completion Phase

Now you can play the fill well in practice, you are up to tempo, your sound is good, and you always know where you are.

Because the fill has now been sorted out, you can add it to your repertoire in the last practice phase.

I suggest you take 5 to 10 minutes per practice session to play without notation. Start the fill at different beats, and play the fill idea over a longer/shorter period of time than you did in the endurance phase.

In principle, you are playing a kind of groove solo with the fill idea.

How to Practice (see Phase 2: Endurance Phase)

At many points throughout the book you'll find practice instructions as to how to work on the exercises when using a metronome. They look like the following:

Practice Steps	
1. Start tempo	Quarter note = 60
2. Number of tempos	3
3. Number of rounds per tempo	Every fill 2 times per tempo
4. Musical form	2-bar groove + 2-bar fill
5. Count out loud	Quarter note and "click"	Sixteenth notes when required
6. Duration of exercise	Around 15 minutes

Explanation

Point 1: The **start tempo** is merely a recommendation. If you feel it is too slow or too fast, choose another tempo!

Point 2: I suggest you play the exercise at three different tempos. In addition to the start tempo of 60, move on to the next two higher tempos from the list below.

Tempo list (bpm)				
60	62	64	66	68
70	73	76	79	
82	85	88		
91	94	97		
100	104	108		
112	116			
120	125			
130	135			
140	145			
150	155			
160	165			
170	175			
180				

Practice the exercise at tempos 60, 62, and 64. Write down the three tempos, and put the date by the highest. When you feel your highest tempo becomes easy to play, take the next fastest tempo and write it on your list. Write the date by the highest tempo, and cross the lowest off your list so you always play in *three* different tempos. The *three tempos* our examples are based on are 60, 62, 64, and 66.

Point 3: The number of rounds per tempo indicates how often you should play each combination of the reading text.

Point 4: In practice, you should always play fills and grooves with one another. Think of the musical form. This means you should think in blocks of four or eight bars.

Point 5 "Count out loud": The most effective way to understand the particular rhythm of each fill in this book is to count out loud! Without keeping a permanent overview of the rhythm in relation to the quarter-note pulse, these exercises are mechanical and unmusical.

It may be laborious at the beginning, but learning the underlying skill will ultimately be useful to you in many different contexts. Unfortunately, playing the quarter note with the left foot on the hi-hat does not replace counting out loud.

My method is explained here using *Example 2* from *Chapter 1* (*see page 12*):

1. Count all the sixteenth notes out loud. This lead-in should make it easier. As soon as that goes well, go ahead with step 2.

Example 2 (Counting: sixteenth notes)

2. Now leave the sixteenth-note subdivision, and only count the quarter notes out loud.
As soon as that goes well, go ahead with step 3.

Example 2.1 (Counting: quarter notes)

3. Now change the counting out loud of the quarter note to a percussive sound:
say "click" for every quarter note.

Example 2.2 (Counting: "Click")

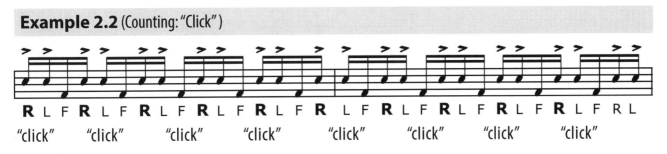

There are two reasons to say "click":

• You have to be more precise than counting, as the sound is much more percussive than saying the numbers.

• Because you don't say the quarter notes out loud anymore, you have to internalize where beat 1 is. When you have internalized this, then you will always hear or feel exactly where you are in the bar.

The Advantages of Practicing This Way

The advantages of practicing this way are:

1. You always start at a tempo that feels really easy.

2. Because this is a clear structure to stick to, you don't need to keep asking yourself if you have practiced for long enough (or too long).

3. By writing down the dates, you can see your progress and know exactly when to cross the exercise off your practice plan. When you feel you don't improve over a long period, leave the exercise and start another.

Drummer **Kim Plainfield** showed me this very systematic way of practicing with a metronome during my residency at the *Drummers Collective* in New York.

Reading Text

The enclosed reading text will be explained in the course of this book and shows different phrasing possibilities you can use to practice later (and should).

And Finally...

Take as much time as you need for all of the exercises in this book. Let it happen slowly and be proud of everything you learn. It's never about learning something quickly. Be guided by your passion and fun, and be diligent and disciplined.

Drumset Notation in This Book

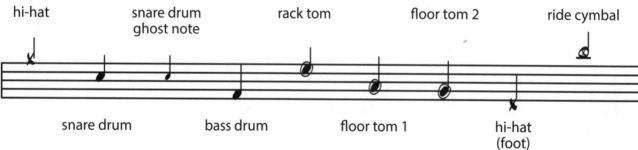

Photo © Marco Hammer

Photo © Elle Jaye

Switch Orchestration, Path Orchestration, Diddle Kick, and More

To start this book, I would like to show you some different ways fills can be expanded upon through *orchestration*(*), *dynamics*, and *doubling* up on strokes. In this way, you can create completely new sounds from motifs you have already learned, but they will hardly be recognized in the same way. You'll play many different fills through clever modification, rather than just by changing the figure.

The best way to get to know these principles is to take a simple figure; the motif for the fills in this chapter is **R L F**, which is very manageable and quite simple.

Fill (Original figure: R L F)

The original figure is three sixteenth notes long, so we'll call it a **3-note grouping**. Play this *over one bar*.

Example 1 (3-note grouping over one bar with the underlying rhythm in line 2)

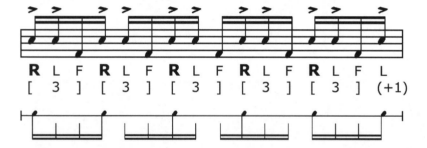

R L F R L F R L F R L F R L F L
[3] [3] [3] [3] [3] (+1)

R = right hand
L = left hand
F = foot

Tip

From time to time you should make the underlying rhythm clear to yourself. How this is accomplished is explained at the beginning of this book on *pages 6 and 7*.

Next, play the 3-note grouping as a *two-bar fill*. The 3-note grouping continues until the end of the two bars.

Example 2 (3-note grouping over two bars)　　　🖸 CD 01

R L F R L F R L F R L F R L F R L F R L F R L F R L F R L F R L
[3] [3] [3] [3] [3] [3] [3] [3] [3] [3] (+ 2)

(*) *Orchestration can be defined as spreading the beats out across the individual parts of the drum kit.*

Count out loud!

In the *preliminary notes,* I explained how I keep track of the fill by making the rhythm especially clear and internalizing it. This is written on *pages 6 and 7.* **It's really important—please read it!**

Now we get to the orchestration of fills. The figure **R L F** stays the same throughout *Chapter 1.*

Switch Orchestration

Three instruments are used in the *Switch Orchestration*(*): you only play the 3-note grouping with the floor tom, hi-hat, and bass drum. In principle, the following happens: the right and left hands swap or "switch" instruments.

In the first exercise, the *right hand* (RH) plays the floor tom and the *left hand* (LH) the hi-hat. The placement remains the same over the *whole two bars.*

Switch Orchestration 1.1 (Preliminary Exercise 1 | RH = floor tom | LH = hi-hat)

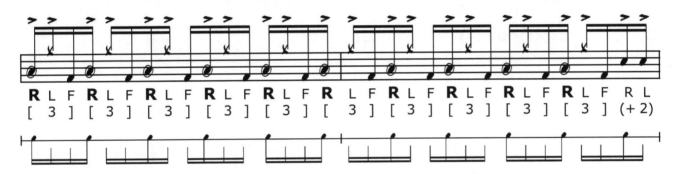

Switch: Now swap the hands: the *right hand* still begins but now plays the hi-hat, whereas the *left hand* plays the floor tom. Therefore the hands are crossed over each other so the right hand is positioned over the left hand.

Switch Orchestration 1.2 (Preliminary Exercise 2 | RH = hi-hat | LH = floor tom)

Practice Tip

You should always practice alternating fills and grooves. Think about the *musical form* in blocks of four or eight bars.

When your fill is a bar long, play three bars of groove and one bar of fill (**3+1**), or seven bars of groove and one bar of fill (**7+1**).

Let's assume your fill is two bars long—then you're either playing two groove cycles plus two bars of fill (**2+2**), or six bars of groove plus two bars of fill (**6+2**).

(*) *Find out more about Switch Orchestration in* **Jost Nickel's Groove Book** *(ISBN 978-3-943638-90-5).*

Now combine exercises 1 and 2:

The first two rounds of the 3-note grouping are played by the *right hand* on the floor tom (LH = hi-hat), followed by two rounds of *Switch*: RH = hi-hat (LH = floor tom).

After playing these *four* rounds, start from the beginning again (marked in **gray notation**).

Switch Orchestration 1.3 (2 x "Normal" and 2 x Switch)

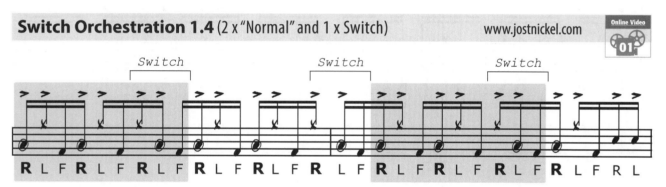

This also sounds really good when you play the "normal" variation *twice* alternated with *one* switch. After these *three rounds*, the orchestration starts from the beginning. You can see this clearly in the *gray markings* of the notation.

Switch Orchestration 1.4 (2 x "Normal" and 1 x Switch)   www.jostnickel.com

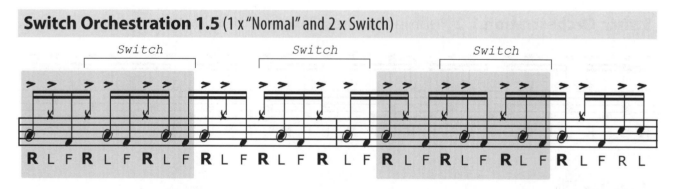

Another good variation to try is to play one of the normal versions followed by *two* of the switches. The orchestration is repeated after *three* rounds of the 3-note grouping.

Switch Orchestration 1.5 (1 x "Normal" and 2 x Switch)

The switch idea works best when limited to two instruments, and the switch is alternated with the "normal" way of playing.

The selection of the instruments you choose to switch will be determined by good accessibility. It is relatively easy to cross your hands over when you play the hi-hat and floor tom. You can and should experiment with other instruments (for example, rack tom and floor tom), but make sure you can always reach them easily!

The *switch orchestration* obviously transfers to other fills. The concept sounds best with fills where the hands only play single strokes.

Orchestration on Snare Drum and Toms

Now it's just a matter of splitting the 3-note grouping between the snare and toms.

It makes sense to think about the general possibilities you have with this—that encourages your imagination and increases your ability to move quickly over the drumset. The aim is for you to share the beats around the toms without needing to think about it.

Our 3-note grouping has a total of four different possibilities as to how the hands can be split around the drums. Above the accents you can see how the strokes are split between toms (T) and snare drum (Sn).

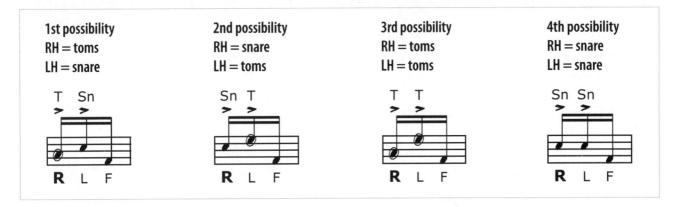

Now combine these four options in a *two-bar fill* by playing each orchestration *twice*. The orchestration is repeated after *eight* rounds of the 3-note grouping.

Snare Drum and Tom Combination 1 (Repeat again after *eight* rounds)

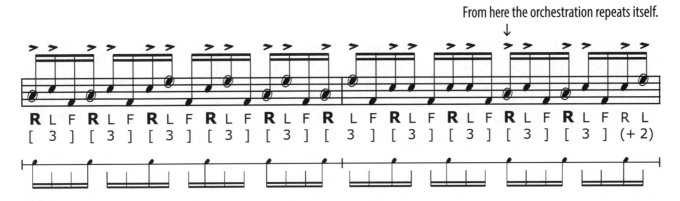

It will be significantly varied when you play the four possibilities *once* next to each other in a *two-bar fill*. The orchestration repeats after four blocks of the 3-note grouping. In the notation, the second round is marked in **gray**, and you can see how the strokes are shared between toms (T) and snare (Sn) above the accents.

Snare Drum and Tom Combination 2 (Repeat after *four* rounds) CD 02

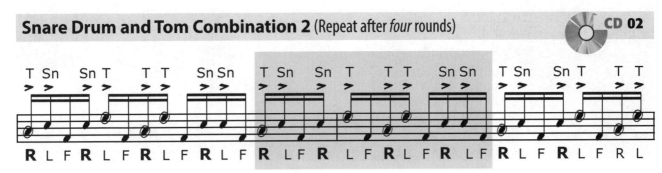

You can also play fills where not all of the possibilities mentioned previously happen. In the following example, the second option is "missing" (snare, toms, bass drum). Because of this, the orchestration is repeated after three rounds of the 3-note grouping.

Snare Drum and Tom Combination 3 (Repeat after *three* rounds)

When you play a possible orchestration twice, the orchestration is repeated after *five* rounds of the group of three.

Snare Drum and Tom Combination 4 (Repeat after *five* rounds)

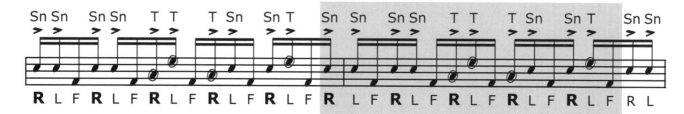

Obviously there are more ways of combining the four orchestration possibilities. I really like it when the orchestrations, as in *Snare Drum and Tom Combinations 1 to 4*, are repeated after a certain number of rounds because the fills then automatically sound like a musical motif, as in opposite to the orchestration being purely coincidental.

Photo © Marco Hammer

Path Orchestration 1

The idea of *Path Orchestration* is that you go to a pre-determined "path" on the set with both hands, with the hands playing a different number of pre-determined instruments.

For example:

The *right hand* plays a loop on *three* instruments: snare drum, rack tom, and floor tom.

The *left hand* plays a loop on *two* instruments: snare drum and rack tom.

Due to the different number of instruments, you will get some very interesting orchestration. The 3-note grouping remains unchanged and is **R L F**.

Here is clarification of the orchestration of the right hand. The left hand is left out of the following example so you have a clearer view of what the right hand does.

Path Orchestration 1.1 (Right hand: snare drum, rack tom, and floor tom)

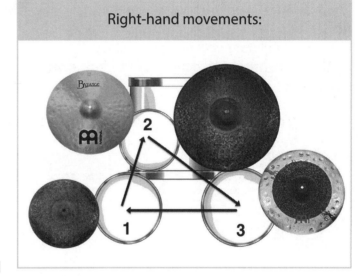

Right-hand movements:

By playing the right hand on three different instruments, the orchestration repeats itself after *three* rounds of the 3-note grouping.

Here is a preliminary exercise so that you feel comfortable with the path in the right hand.

Play the 3-note grouping over two bars, where the right hand—as described earlier—keeps alternating between snare drum, rack tom, and floor tom, while the left hand stays on the snare drum, for the moment. From the **gray markings**, you can see where the orchestration starts from the beginning.

Path Orchestration 1.2 (Preliminary right-hand path exercise)

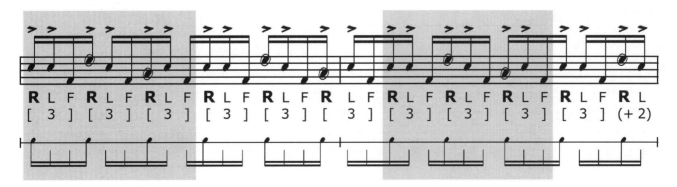

Now let's move on to the orchestration of the *left hand*. This repeats itself after *two* rounds as the left hand plays *two* different instruments (*snare and rack tom*).

Path Orchestration 1.3 (Left hand: snare drum and rack tom)

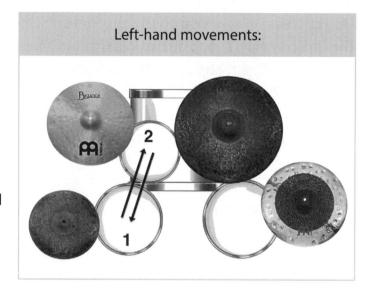

Left-hand movements:

Here is a preliminary exercise so that you feel comfortable with the path in the left hand.

You play **R L F** over two bars, where the *left hand* alternates between snare drum and rack tom, while the *right hand* now stays on the snare drum. From the **gray markings**, you can see where the orchestration starts from the beginning.

Path Orchestration 1.4 (Preliminary left-hand path exercise)

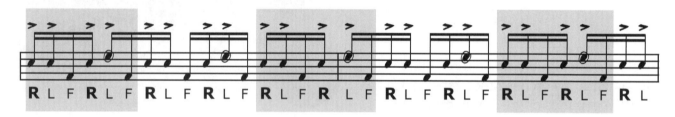

Now let's add both together to create a *two-bar fill*. Try to memorize the fill so you play it by heart. Let the various paths that your hands go to on the set really sink in, and then play the 3-note grouping.

Here are the *directions*: Both hands start on the snare drum, then move to the rack tom at the same time, and then separate and go their own way. The right hand goes to the floor tom and the left hand goes back to the snare drum. If the right hand is on the snare drum, the left hand is already back on the rack tom, etc.

The orchestration repeats itself after you've played the 3-note grouping six times. For the sake of being thorough, here is the notated fill:

Path Orchestration 1.5

www.jostnickel.com

From here the orchestration repeats itself.
↓

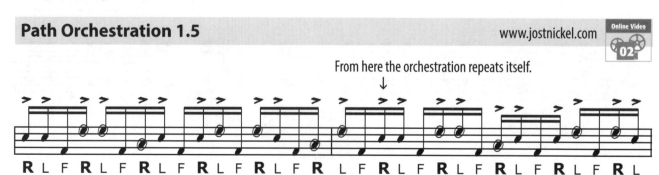

Path Orchestration 2

Next let's extend the *Path Orchestration*. The *right hand* now plays a path over *four* instruments: snare drum, floor tom, ride cymbal, and rack tom.

The *left hand* plays a path on *three* instruments: snare drum, hi-hat, and rack tom.

Here's clarification of the *right hand's orchestration*. The *left hand* is left out of the following notated example so you have a clearer view of what the right hand does.

Path Orchestration 2.1 (Right hand: snare drum, floor tom, ride cymbal, and rack tom)

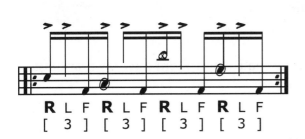

Right-hand movements:

As the right hand plays *four* different instruments, the orchestration repeats itself after *four rounds of the 3-note grouping*.

Here is a preliminary exercise so you feel comfortable with the path of the right hand.

You play **R L F** over two bars, where the *right hand*—as previously explained—always alternates between snare drum, floor tom, ride cymbal, and rack tom, while the *left hand* stays on the snare drum. From the **gray markings**, you can see where the orchestration starts from the beginning.

Path Orchestration 2.2

Now let's move to the orchestration of the *left hand*. This repeats itself after *three* rounds as the left hand only plays *three* different instruments (snare drum, hi-hat, and rack tom).

Path Orchestration 2.3 (Left hand: snare drum, hi-hat, and rack tom)

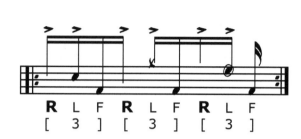

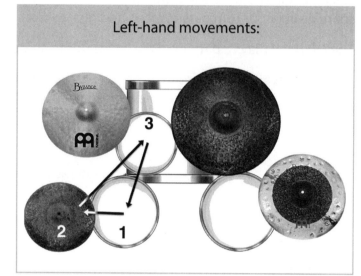

Left-hand movements:

Here is a preliminary exercise so you feel comfortable with the path of the left hand.

Play the 3-note grouping over two bars, where the *left hand* alternates between snare drum, hi-hat, and rack tom, while the *right hand* stays on the snare drum. From the **gray markings**, you can see where the orchestration starts from the beginning.

Path Orchestration 2.4 (Preliminary left-hand path exercise)

Now add both together to make a *two-bar fill*. Again, try to memorize the fill and play it by heart. Let the various paths your hands go to on the set really sink in, then play **R L F**.

Theoretically, the orchestration repeats itself after you have played **R L F** twelve times. However, it doesn't come to this in a *two-bar fill*.

For the sake of being thorough, here's the notated fill:

Path Orchestration 2.5

www.jostnickel.com

Path Orchestration can, of course, be transferred to other fills. The concept sounds best when the hands play single strokes exclusively.

Dynamics 1: Accents

Just by adding or removing accents (Wikipedia definition of accent: *"'an emphasis using louder sound or a stronger articulation'"*), you can make the lovely **R L F** fill sound completely different and good! In the following fills, both hands play the snare drum. The fills only differ in their accents.

In all the previous fills in this chapter, both the right and left hands were accented. Now only accent the first beat, and then play the second beat quietly. The bass-drum beat at the end should be about as loud as the accent in the figure.

Accent 1 (Original figure–1st beat = right hand accented)

With this accent, now play the 3-note grouping over *two bars*.

Accent 2 (1st beat = right hand accented)

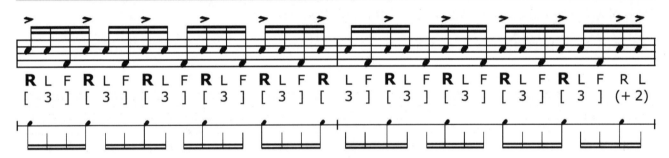

Next, only accent the *second beat* and play the first beat quietly.

Accent 3 (2nd beat = left hand accented)

Now play this accent over *two bars* as well.

Accent 4 (2nd beat = left hand accented)

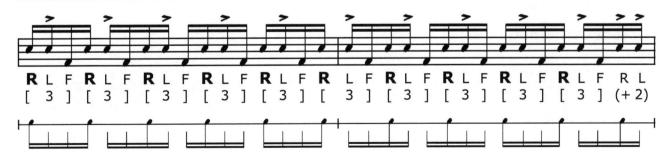

So, there are only the following two ways of accenting one stroke of the figure.

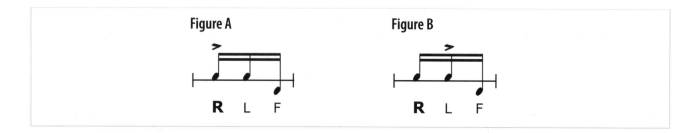

If you combine **Figures A** and **B**, it creates some very interesting accentuation. Keep *alternating* between Figure A and Figure B in the following fill.

Accent Combination 1 (A and B alternated)

Now play figure A *twice*, followed by *twice* through figure B.

Accent Combination 2 (2 x A and 2 x B)

It sounds particularly nice if you only play one of the figures twice.
The next combination shows figure A played *two times*, followed by figure B played *one time*.

Accent Combination 3 (2 x A and 1 x B)   CD 03

And now figure A played *once* followed by figure B played *twice*.

Accent Combination 4 (1 x A and 2 x B)

Practice Tip

In principle, the playing of concrete, pre-determined accents is only an intermediate step. In order to be able to play accents freely, improvise by practicing the various accents over one or two bars.

This is an improvisation in a very narrow context. The figure (**R L F**) and the orchestration (snare drum and bass drum) are fixed. You only change the accents in your improvisation.

Photo © Drumeo

Diddle Kick

Diddle means a double stroke. *Diddle kick* means a double stroke on the bass drum.

A diddle kick (almost) always sounds good, if an original figure only contains single bass-drum beats. This is the case with our 3-note grouping. You are now playing two 32nd notes in the bass drum instead of a sixteenth note. The hands remain unchanged.

So here is the well-known 3-note grouping with a diddle kick over *two bars*. Both hands stay on the snare drum.

Diddle Kick 1 (*All* bass-drum beats are doubled)   www.jostnickel.com

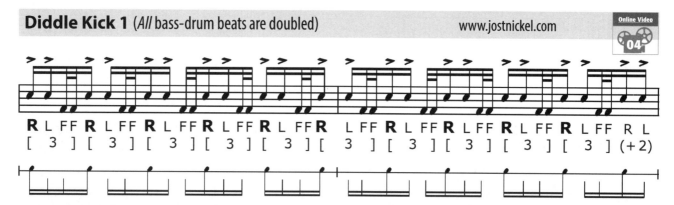

Practice Tip

If you have a double pedal, you can share both the bass-drum beats between your feet. I play the first beat with my *right* foot and then the second with my *left*.

However, I almost always play both beats with the *right* foot (and would also recommend that to double-pedal players as well). In order to be able to play both double strokes quickly with one foot, I slide the right foot over the pedal. The sliding motion is in the direction of the bass-drum skin. You can see it well in the *Video*.

As always, less is more. Now every second bass-drum beat will be *doubled*. The resulting figure is repeated after *two rounds* of the 3-note grouping (*see the* **gray marking**).

Diddle Kick 2 (Every *second* bass-drum beat is doubled)

Sometimes even less is even more. Now only the *third* bass-drum beat will be doubled. The resulting figure repeats itself after *three rounds* of the 3-note grouping (*see the* **gray marking**).

Diddle Kick 3 (Every *third* bass-drum beat is doubled)

Diddle Kick with Switch Orchestration

Next, combine the *diddle kick* with the *switch orchestration.* Play *Switch Orchestration 1.4 (see page 14)* and double all bass-drum beats.

To recap: In *Switch Orchestration 1.4,* play the "normal" variation twice, followed by one switch. The resulting figure repeats itself after *three* rounds of the 3-note grouping *(see the **gray marking**)*.

Diddle Kick 4 (Diddle Kick with Switch Orchestration 1.4)   www.jostnickel.com

Diddle Kick with Path Orchestration

Path Orchestration works perfectly for doubling bass-drum beats as well. Play *Path Orchestration 1.5 (see page 18)*, and double all of the bass-drum beats.

To recap: In *Path Orchestration 1.5,* both hands play their repeating paths:
The *right hand* plays a path over three instruments (snare drum, rack tom, and floor tom), while the *left hand* plays a path over two instruments (snare drum and rack tom).

The orchestration repeats itself after you have played the 3-note grouping *six times.*

Diddle Kick 5 (Diddle Kick with Path Orchestration 1.5)   CD 04

From here the orchestration repeats itself.

Dynamics 2: Dynamic Levels

The last part of this chapter deals with the abrupt transition between two extremely different levels of dynamics. This should be exaggerated for practice purposes (e.g., very quiet and very loud).

The control over the different dynamic levels will greatly contribute to the versatility of your playing. Your fills (and grooves) will become more interesting and sound more musical.

In the notation, the parts of the fills that should be played quietly are small, and the parts of the fill that should be loud are big.

With all dynamic levels it is really important that you watch out for the volume of your bass drum!

First play the 3-note grouping *quietly* in bar 1 and *loudly* in bar 2.

Dynamic Levels 1.1 (Bar 1: quiet–bar 2: loud)

The transition between the two dynamic levels splits the 3-note grouping at the bar line:
The *right hand* is *quiet* on the last sixteenth note of the first bar, but the *left hand* is then *loud* on beat 1 of the second bar.

The next exercise is the opposite of *Dynamic Levels 1.1*: The first bar here is *loud*, and the second is *quiet*.

Dynamic Levels 1.2 (Bar 1: loud–bar 2: quiet)

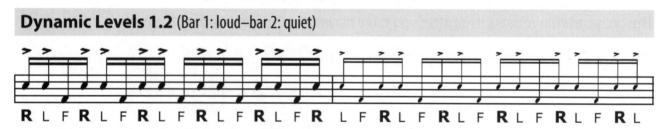

Now the dynamic steps get shorter. Play the fill *quietly* over *three quarter notes*, and then *loudly* over *three quarter notes* until two bars are complete.

Dynamic Levels 2.1 (3 quarter notes: quiet–3 quarter notes: loud–2 quarter notes: quiet)

The next exercise works the opposite. The principle is the same as for *Dynamic Levels 2.1*, but you start loudly.

Dynamic Levels 2.2 (3 quarter notes: loud 3 quarter notes: quiet–2 quarter notes: loud)

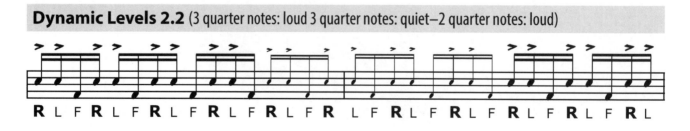

The dynamic steps get even shorter. Now you only stay at each level for *two quarter notes*.

Dynamic Levels 3.1 (Alternating between 2 quarter notes: quiet–2 quarter notes: loud)

R L F R L F R L F R L F R L F R L F R L F R L F R L F R L

The next exercise works the opposite. The principle is the same as in *Dynamic Levels 3.1*, but you start *loudly*.

Dynamic Levels 3.2 (Alternating between 2 quarter notes: loud–2 quarter notes: quiet)

R L F R L F R L F R L F R L F R L F R L F R L F R L F R L

You guessed it—the dynamic levels get even shorter.

Now you only stay at each level for *one quarter note* long. *Dynamic Levels 4.1* begins *quietly*, whereas *Dynamic Levels 4.2* begins *loudly*.

The shorter the dynamic levels are, the harder they are to play. Pay attention to abrupt transitions.

Dynamic Levels 4.1 (Alternating between 1 quarter note: quiet–1 quarter note: loud)

R L F R L F R L F R L F R L F R L F R L F R L F R L F R L

Dynamic Levels 4.2 (Alternating between 1 quarter note: loud–1 quarter note: quiet)

R L F R L F R L F R L F R L F R L F R L F R L F R L F R L

Now we'll apply the dynamic levels to the *3-note grouping*. That means you play the 3-note grouping *three times quietly*, followed by *three times loudly* until the two bars are complete.

Dynamic Levels 5.1 (3-note grouping: 3 times quiet–3 times loud)

R L F R L F R L F R L F R L F R L F R L F R L F R L F R L

Dynamic Levels 5.2 works the opposite:
Play the 3-note grouping *three times loudly*, followed by *three times quietly*.

Dynamic Levels 5.2 (3-note grouping: 3 times loud–3 times quiet)

The dynamic levels are still derived from the 3-note grouping but are shorter.
Now play the 3-note grouping *twice quietly*, followed by *twice loudly*.

Dynamic Levels 6.1 (3-note grouping: 2 times quiet–2 times loud)

Dynamic Levels 6.2 works the opposite:
Play the 3-note grouping *twice loudly*, followed by *twice quietly*.

Dynamic Levels 6.2 (3-note grouping: 2 times loud–2 times quiet)

And, what shouldn't be left out at the end? That the 3-note grouping is played *once quietly* and *once loudly* until the two bars are complete.

Dynamic Levels 7.1 (3-note grouping: 1 time quiet–1 time loud)

Dynamic Levels 7.2 works the opposite:
Play the 3-note grouping *one time loud*, followed by *one quiet* 3-note grouping.

Dynamic Levels 7.2 (3-note grouping: 1 time loud–1 time quiet)

All exercises in this part of the chapter refer to abrupt dynamic changes. You should also practice gradual changes in the volume of a fill. Here are three examples:

1. Your fill starts quietly, gets gradually louder, and ends as loudly as possible:

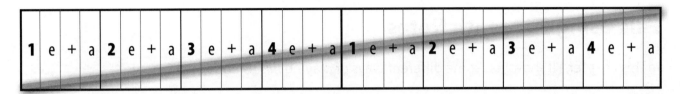

2. The opposite:
   Your fill starts loudly, gets gradually quieter, and ends as quietly as possible:

3. You play wave-like dynamics. Start loudly, go louder, go quiet, etc. until the end of the fill:

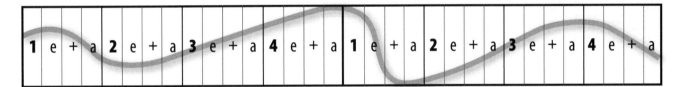

Practice Tip

As dynamic-level exercises are often neglected, I recommend you include these exercises in your practice plan. *Dynamic Levels 1.1 to 4.2* can be transferred to all other fills.

If you practice daily in this way, *5 to 10 minutes* a day is enough.

If you can play the exercises well, you should also experiment with less varied dynamics (e.g., loud and very loud).

Fills Using Sixteenth Notes

In this chapter, I'll show you some different ways of playing *fills using sixteenth notes*.

Fills Using Sixteenth Notes 1 (4- and 2-Note Groupings)

First play a figure that is one quarter note long. In sixteenth notes that is *four* beats.

Sixteenth-Note Fill (Original figure: R L L F)

Sixteenth-Note Fill 1 (Original figure: R L L F over a whole bar)

As the initial figure is four sixteenth notes, it's now called the *4-note grouping*.

Make sure you play both the unaccented notes softly in the left hand. The bass-drum beat at the end should be about as loud as the accent at the beginning.

Internalizing New Motifs

First, become familiar with the motions of a fill by playing it several times without reference to the pulse. It can be helpful to speed up and slow down while playing the fill.

Once you have internalized the new fill, you should always play at a specific tempo and be aware of the quarter-note pulse.

You can make the 4-note grouping sound different by moving it one eighth note in the bar from the *downbeat* to the *offbeat*[(*)]. The challenge is as follows:

Start the fill on beat 1+, and listen to how different it sounds in relation to the quarter-note pulse.

Theoretically, you could start the 4-note grouping on each of the four sixteenth notes. Now, however, we're concentrating on the shift of an eighth note, and we'll let the other possibilities slide for the moment. On beat 1, play a snare-drum accent and then the 4-note grouping from beat 1+:

[(*)] *An offbeat is the even space in between the counts of a metronome.*

Sixteenth-Note Fill 2 (4-note grouping displaced by an eighth note)

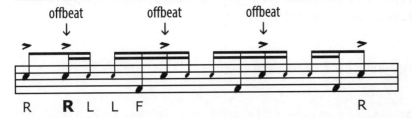

Now we will add both sixteenth-note fills together to make a *two-bar fill*. Play the 4-note grouping on the downbeat in *bar 1*, and then switch to the offbeat for *bar 2* (*see arrows*).

You can see the underlying rhythm of the fills for clarity in *line 2*.

Sixteenth-Note Fills 1 & 2 (Combination)

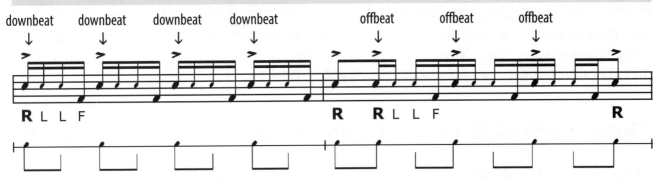

Eighth notes are the underlying rhythm of the 4- and 2-note groupings. To internalize them, here are two different approaches using the *Sixteenth-Note Fills 1 & 2* (*see above*). This approach can be used with all fills that have an underlying rhythm of eighth notes.

1. Play the fill in **bars 1 and 2**. In **bars 3 and 4**, play eighth notes on the snare drum with the *right hand*, and emphasize the rhythm. At the same time, play the quarter-note pulse with the hi-hat pedal to further enhance your understanding.

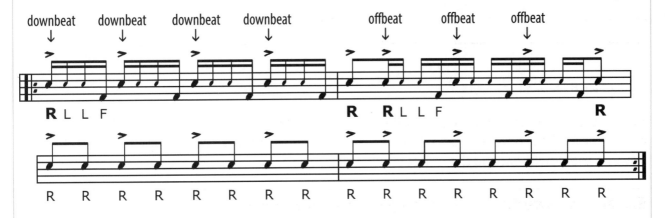

2. In **bars 1 and 2**, play the fill and in **bars 3 and 4**, play a groove with the underlying rhythm as a bass-drum figure:

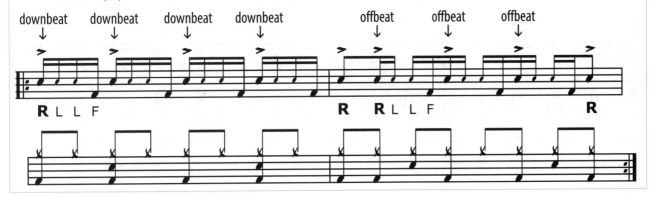

Next we need a more elegant transition between the two positions of the original figure. Instead of the eighth notes on the snare drum (*see page 31, Sixteenth-Note Fills 1 & 2, bar 2, beats 1 and 4+*), *play the following two sixteenth notes, which are an eighth note long together.*

Sixteenth-Note Fill 3 (Transition snare drum, bar 2, beats 1 and 4+)

The transition is over two sixteenth notes and is therefore called the *2-note grouping*.

Insert the 2-note grouping into the combined two-bar *Sixteenth-Note Fills 1 & 2* (*see page 31*).
Start the fill with the 4-note grouping on beat 1 (the downbeat). On beat 1 of the second bar, play the 2-note grouping *once*, directly followed by the 4-note grouping, which now starts on the *offbeat* (beat 1+). At the end, the 2-note grouping is played on beat 4+.

Sixteenth-Note Fill 4 (4- and 2-note groupings | Combination 1)

CD 05

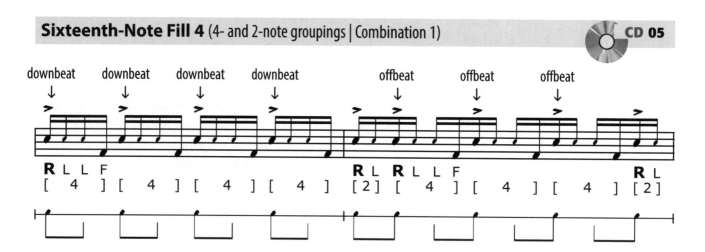

Now it gets even more rhythmically interesting. You're going to keep changing between the 4-note grouping and the 2-note grouping. As a result, the position of the 4-note grouping always changes between the downbeat and the offbeat.

Sixteenth-Note Fill 5 (4- and 2-note groupings | Combination 2)

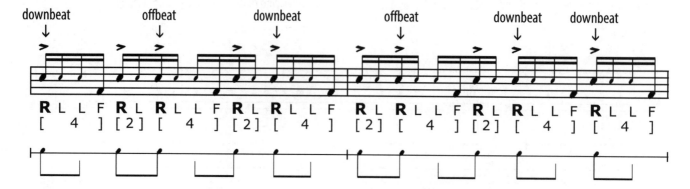

The next example shows another possible combination of the 4- and 2-note groupings. Here you start with the 2-note grouping (i.e., the first 4-note grouping starts on the offbeat).

Sixteenth-Note Fill 6 (4- and 2-note groupings | Combination 3)

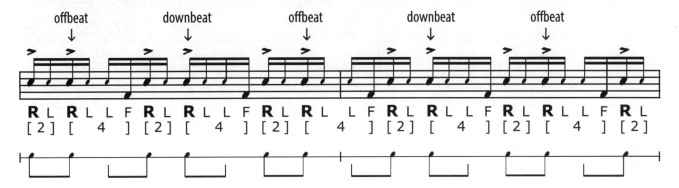

Cross-Reference

In the *Appendix, on page 131,* you will find a snare-drum exercise that also combines 4- and 2-note groupings. The aim of this snare-drum exercise is to further the basic rhythmic idea so it can be more easily controlled and transferred to other motifs. I mostly play snare-drum exercises on my practice pad. Specifically, you can practice the snare exercise on the pad first (possibly to warm up) and then play the fill on the set. Play these exercises at a moderate tempo. It is mainly about understanding the underlying rhythm.

The best thing about working with groups is that they can be used for improvisation. In order to do this, you have to play the figures by heart and (more importantly) be able to hear the underlying rhythm in relation to the quarter-note pulse.

Improvising means playing without notation.

Try to play the next two fills just by using the numbers (in *square brackets* below the notation) so you can gradually get rid of the notes. I've omitted the sticking because hopefully you know it by now. The notes are still there in case you need a visual.

[4] = R L L F

[2] = R L

Sixteenth-Note Fill 7 (4- and 2-note groupings | Combination 4)

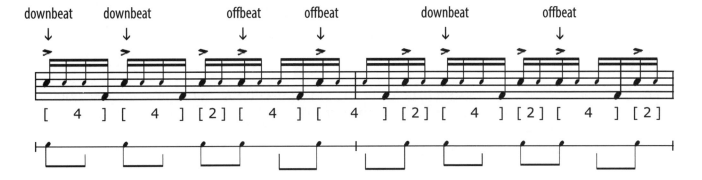

Sixteenth-Note Fill 8 (4- and 2-note groupings | Combination 5)

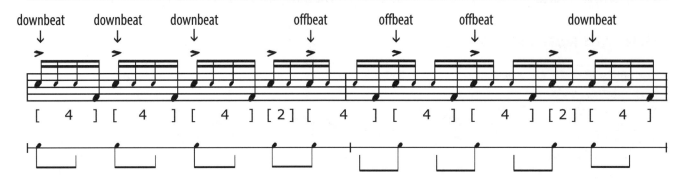

In order to become rhythmically more certain in dealing with the 4- and 2-note groupings, you should practice further combinations in accordance with this principle. To do this, you need to work with place holders (the numbers 4 and 2). The following four combinations of the 4- and 2-note groupings each represent a *two-bar fill* in $\frac{4}{4}$ time.

The counting is in the *second line* so you know where you are.

Sixteenth-Note Fill 9 (4- and 2-note groupings | Combination 6)

4		2	4		4		2	4		4		2	4		2
1	+	2	+	3	+	4	+	1	+	2	+	3	+	4	+

Sixteenth-Note Fill 10 (4- and 2-note groupings | Combination 7)

2	4		4		4		2	4		4		2	4		2	
1	+	2	+	3	+	4	+	1	+	2	+	3	+	4	+

Sixteenth-Note Fill 11 (4- and 2-note groupings | Combination 8)

2	4		2	2	4		2	4		2	4		4		2
1	+	2	+	3	+	4	+	1	+	2	+	3	+	4	+

Sixteenth-Note Fill 12 (4- and 2-note groupings | Combination 9)

4		4		2	2	2	4		2	2	4		2	4	
1	+	2	+	3	+	4	+	1	+	2	+	3	+	4	+

The Principle

Play the *4-note grouping using sixteenth notes*. In combination with the *2-note grouping*, the *4-note grouping* changes between the *downbeat* and the *offbeat*.

Subdivision[*] of fills: **Sixteenth notes**

Grid of underlying rhythm: **Eighth notes**

---

[*] *Subdivision = the rhythmic division of the basis of a note value*

And so it continues:

Now practice all the two-bar combinations with the help of the instructions below (explained in detail in the *Preliminary Notes*).

This works best with **Reading Text 1** (*4- and 2-Note Groupings Using Sixteenth Notes*), where all combinations (*Sixteenth-Note Fills 4–12*) are clearly written on one page.

Practice Steps	
Start tempo	Quarter note = 60
Number of tempos	3
Number of rounds per tempo	Every fill 2 times per tempo
Musical form	2-bar groove + 2-bar fill
Count out loud	Quarter note and "click"	sixteenth notes when required
Duration of exercise	Around 15 minutes

Tips for Improvisation

Playing by numbers is great but it should only be an intermediate step on the way to being free with these fills. As soon as you can play the combinations well and know where the pulse and beat 1 are, you can start to improvise. At first, stick with the *two-bar fills*, and improvise using different combinations from the 4- and 2-note groupings.

Improvising means that when you play you don't think about counting or groups anymore. Instead, you hear the rhythmic structure all the time and can be free with the material.

Photo © Mario Schmitt

As you've now mastered the rhythmic concept (*4-and 2-note groupings*), you should transfer it to other motifs. Here is an example:

"Foot Swap" Orchestration Concept

Instead of the bass drum, play the hi-hat (pedal) with the *left foot*. Now, play the next beat with the *right hand* on the hi-hat (so the pedaled hi-hat is directly followed by the played hi-hat). This concept can be applied to ALL fills with a single bass-drum beat. The 4- and 2-note groupings we've used so far are thus slightly changed and will now look like this:

Foot Swap (Original figure)

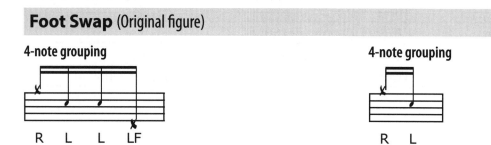

Now combine the 4- and 2-note groupings with **Reading Text 1** (*4- and 2-Note Groupings Using Sixteenth Notes*). For the sake of clarity, here's *Combination 1* of the reading text as the basis for the following fill:

Foot Swap 1 (Combination 1 from Reading Text 1)   CD 07

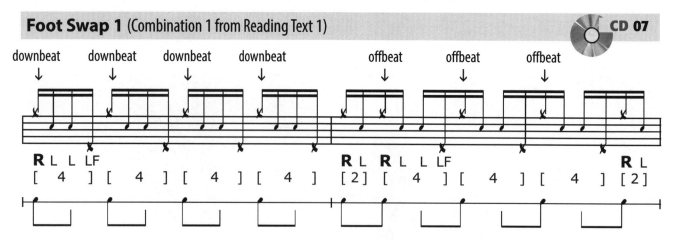

As you can see, this rhythmic principle can be applied in many different ways. Make up your own 4- and 2-note groupings!

I recommend that you check out the following rhythmic concepts in this book and then return to the *4- and 2-Note Groupings Using Sixteenth Notes* later.

Practice Steps	
Start tempo	Quarter note = 70
Number of tempos	3
Number of rounds per tempo	Every fill 2 times per tempo
Musical form	2-bar groove + 2-bar fill
Count out loud	Quarter note and "click" | sixteenth notes when required
Duration of exercise	Around 15 minutes

Fills Using Sixteenth Notes 2 (Displaced 4- and 2-Note Groupings)

Now you're going to increase your rhythmic flexibility and the possibilities for expression by displacing the well-known 4-note grouping by *one* sixteenth note.

Continue to play **R L L F**, but start one sixteenth note earlier:

Sixteenth-Note Fill 2.1 (Original figure | R L L F one sixteenth note earlier)

Here's the figure from *Example 2.1* over a bar with the underlying rhythm in *line 2*.

Sixteenth-Note Fill 2.2 (Original figure = 4-note grouping over one bar)   CD 08

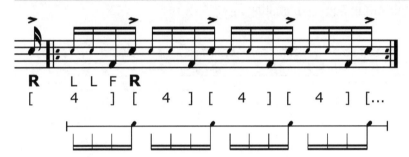

It also sounds really good when you begin the 4-note grouping (**R L L F**) one sixteenth note after beat 1.

Sixteenth-Note Fill 2.3 (4-note grouping one sixteenth note later)   CD 09

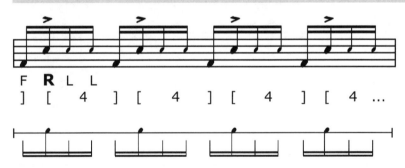

In the next step, add the *2-note grouping* you already know. This is also displaced by one sixteenth note and has two accents now.

Sixteenth-Note Fill 2.4 (2-note grouping)

On the following page, combine the 4- and 2-note groupings.

In the 2-note grouping, *both hands* are accented. The accent in the left hand always lands exactly on the eighth note (marked in **gray** in *bar 2* of each of the following fills). As a result, the fill, which has been displaced by one sixteenth note, still sounds good and is easier to hear.

Sixteenth-Note Fill 2.5 (4- and 2-note groupings | Combination 1)   **CD 10**

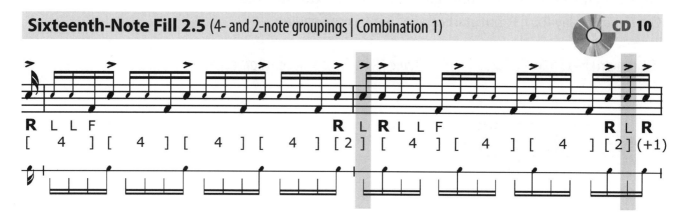

In both of the following fills, the accented left hand is shown in **gray**.

Sixteenth-Note Fill 2.6 (4- and 2-note groupings | Combination 2)

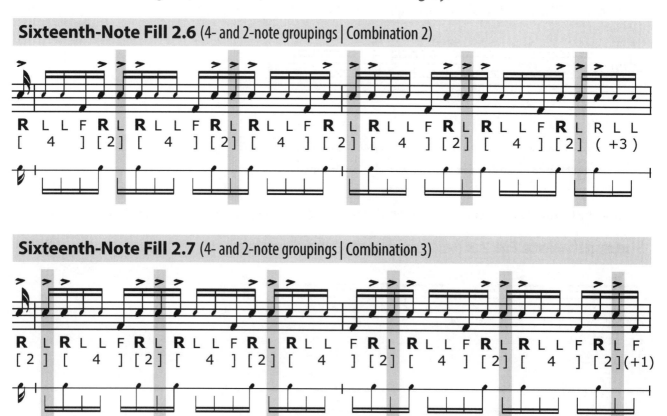

Sixteenth-Note Fill 2.7 (4- and 2-note groupings | Combination 3)

If you have practiced all of the fills using sixteenth notes and don't have any problems counting out loud, you can now continue combining all of the previously played positions of the 4-note grouping with each other.

Fills Using Sixteenth Notes 3 (4- and 3-Note Groupings)

Now you're going to play all four positions of the 4-note groupings in one fill. To do this, combine the *4-note grouping* with the *3-note grouping*.

For the 3-note grouping, play the figure from *Chapter 1* you already know: **R L F.**

Both hands are accented.

Sixteenth-Note Fill 3.1 (3-note grouping)

The first combination is over *four bars*. All four possible positions of the 4-note grouping come within these four bars. The 3-note groupings are marked in **gray**. The underlying rhythm can be seen in *lines 2* and *4*.

Sixteenth-Note Fill 3.2 (4- and 3-note groupings over four bars)   CD 11

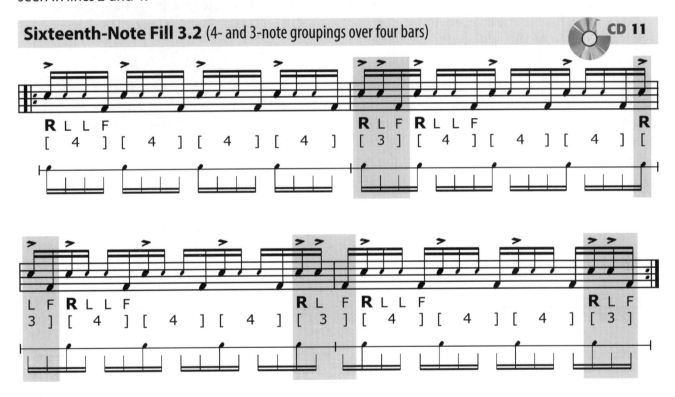

Now we come to *two-bar fills* with 4- and 3-note groupings. When playing *Sixteenth-Note Fill 3.3*, always play alternating 4- and 3-note groupings (marked in **gray**). As a result, the 4-note grouping always moves forward by a sixteenth note.

Sixteenth-Note Fill 3.3 (4- and 3-note groupings | Combination 1)

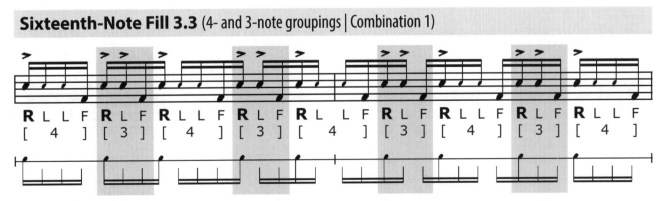

Continue with alternating 4- and 3-note groupings. Now begin with the 3-note grouping:

Sixteenth-Note Fill 3.4 (4- and 3-note groupings | Combination 2)

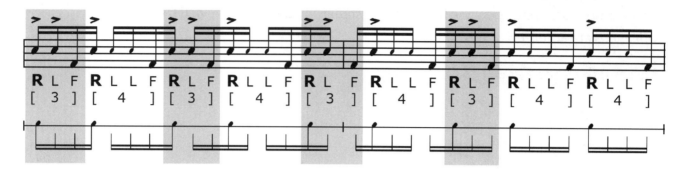

Cross-Reference

There is a snare exercise in the *Appendix* on the subject of 4- and 3-note groupings (*see page 132*). The aim is to further the basic rhythmic idea here as well. It will be useful to practice the snare-drum exercises and fills within the same practice session.

As you already know, the combinations of groups are perfect for improvising. In order to do that, you need to be able to play the figures by heart and hear the underlying rhythm in relation to the quarter-note pulse. Try to play the next two fills just by the numbers (in *square brackets* below the notation) so you can gradually get rid of the notes.

Because you know the sticking already, I've left it out of the following examples. The notes are still there in case you need a visual.

The best thing to do is to pay attention to the numbers in the *square brackets*!

[4] = R L L F

[3] = R L F

Sixteenth-Note Fill 3.5 (4- and 3-note groupings | Combination 3)

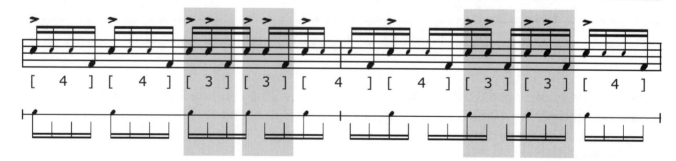

Sixteenth-Note Fill 3.6 (4- and 3-note groupings | Combination 4)

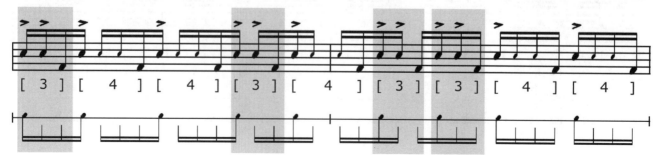

To become absolutely certain when dealing with the 4- and 3-note groupings, you should practice further combinations. As the stickings are now known, the only thing new will be to practice different combinations. To do this, you need to work with place holders (the numbers 4 and 3). The following four combinations of the 4- and 3-note groupings each represent a *two-bar fill* in $\frac{4}{4}$ time. So you know where you are, you can find the counting in the *second line*.

Sixteenth-Note Fill 3.7 (4- and 3-note groupings | Combination 5) CD 12

Sixteenth-Note Fill 3.8 (4- and 3-note groupings | Combination 6)

In the following examples, *3.9* and *3.10*, you will see "+2" at the end. That means two sixteenth notes will be missing until two bars are complete. You simply play **R L** here.

Sixteenth-Note Fill 3.9 (4- and 3-note groupings | Combination 7)

Sixteenth-Note Fill 3.10 (4- and 3-note groupings | Combination 8)

3	3	3	4	3	4	3	4	3	+2
1 e + a	2 e + a	3 e + a	4 e + a	1 e + a	2 e + a	3 e + a	4 e + a		

Orchestration Tip: Bring the toms into play by playing the floor tom with the *right hand* and the rack tom with the *left* in all 3-note groupings. The 4-note grouping orchestration remains unchanged.

The Principle

Play the *4-note grouping using sixteenth notes*. By combining them with the *3-note grouping*, you will play them in all four positions.

Subdivision of fills: **Sixteenth notes**
Grid of underlying rhythm: **Sixteenth notes**

And so it continues:

Now practice all two-bar combinations using the instructions below (explained in detail in the *Preliminary Notes*).

This works best with **Reading Text 2** (*4- and 3-Note Groupings Using Sixteenth Notes*). There you will find an overview of all combinations (*examples 3.3–3.10*).

Practice Steps	
Start tempo	Quarter note = 70
Number of tempos	3
Number of rounds per tempo	Every fill 2 times per tempo
Musical form	2-bar groove + 2-bar fill
Count out loud	Quarter note and "click" | sixteenth notes when required
Duration of exercise	Around 15 minutes

This rhythmic concept (*4- and 3-note groupings*) transfers well to other motifs.

For example:

Play the 4-note grouping with two bass-drum beats. The 3-note grouping stays the same.

"Two Bass-Drum Beats" 1 (Original figures)

4-note grouping

R   L   F   F

3-note grouping

R   L   F

Now combine the 4- and 3-note groupings with **Reading Text 2** (*4- and 3-Note Groupings Using Sixteenth Notes*). For the sake of clarity, here's *combination 1* of the reading text as the basis for the following fill.

"Two Bass-Drum Beats" 2 (Combination 1 from Reading Text 2) ◉ CD 13

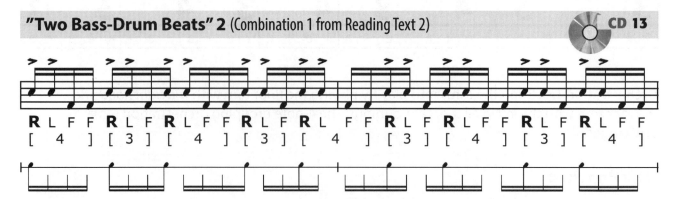

To make the transition from the above fill back in to the groove a little easier, replace the last bass-drum beat with a left-hand beat. Then you can comfortably play a bass drum on the next beat 1.

When practicing the other combinations from **Reading Text 2**, also play the toms instead of the snare drum.

Practice Steps	
Start tempo	Quarter note = 70
Number of tempos	3
Number of rounds per tempo	Every fill 2 times per tempo
Musical form	2-bar groove + 2-bar fill
Count out loud	Quarter note and "click"	sixteenth notes when required
Duration of exercise	Around 15 minutes

On the topic of orchestration:

The *Path Orchestration* concept, explained in *Chapter 1*, *pages 17 to 20*, can be transferred to these 4- and 3-note groupings, since the hands play single strokes here. This is to remind you of the paths you played in *Path Orchestration 1*:

The *right hand* plays a loop
on *three* instruments:
snare drum, rack tom, and floor tom

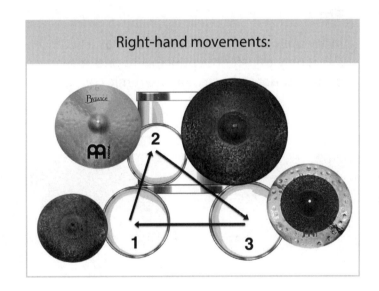

The *left hand* plays a loop
on *two* instruments:
snare drum and rack tom

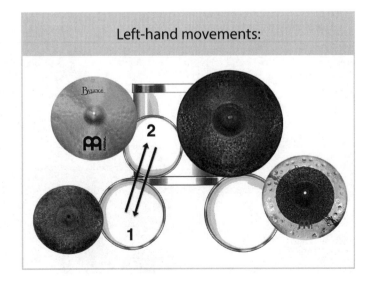

When you transfer *Path Orchestration 1* to the *"Two Bass-Drum Beats"* 2 example *(Combination 1 from Reading Text 2)*, it looks like this:

www.jostnickel.com

"Two Bass-Drum Beats" 3 (Combination 1 from Reading Text 2 with Path Orchestration 1)

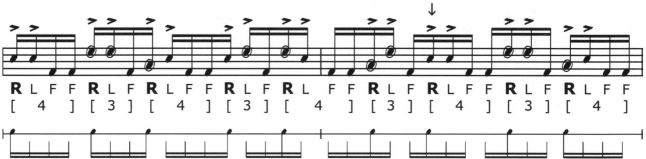

To make the transition from the above fill back in to the groove a little easier, replace the last bass-drum beat with a left-hand beat. Then you can comfortably play a bass drum on the next beat 1.

Tip

In my opinion, it isn't necessary to play all combinations with the path orchestration. It's enough if you only transfer the principle to one or two combinations. Now, simply continue with this book in order to learn more rhythmic concepts and ways to implement them.

Photo © Elle Jaye

Fills Using Sixteenth Notes 4 (4- and 1-Note Groupings)

Here is a simple but effective way of creating a rhythm I can't leave unmentioned. Again, it is about playing all four positions of the 4-note grouping in a fill. To do this, combine the 4-note groupings with 1-note groupings in a four-bar fill. (You can't talk about a "group" of one note, of course, but I hope you know what I mean.)

Our 1-note grouping is an accented beat with the left hand and is marked in **gray**.

Sixteenth-Note Fill 4.1 (4- and 1-note groupings over four bars)

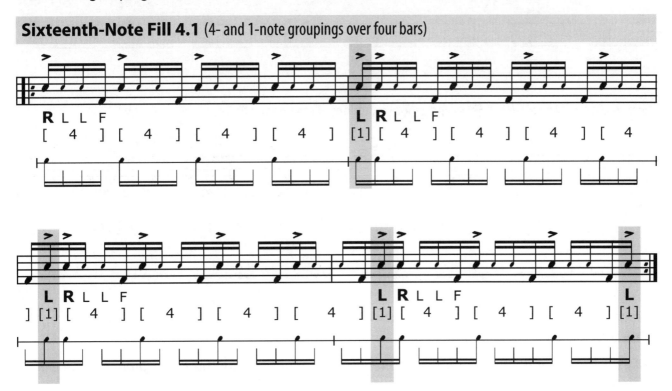

Now we come to two-bar combination fills.

Sixteenth-Note Fill 4.2 (4- and 1-note groupings | Combination 1)   CD 14

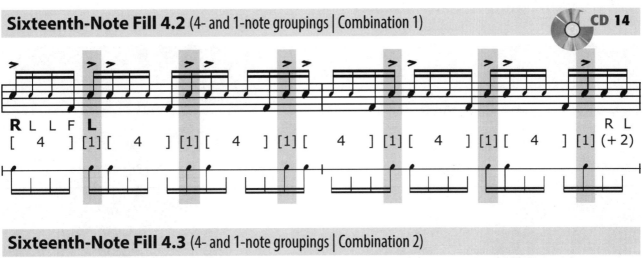

Sixteenth-Note Fill 4.3 (4- and 1-note groupings | Combination 2)

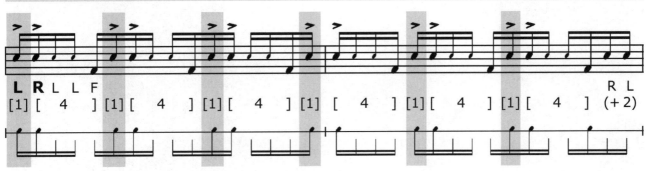

45

Sixteenth-Note Fill 4.4 (4- and 1-note groupings | Combination 3)

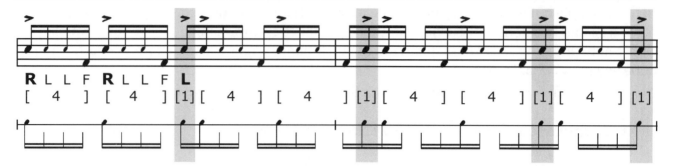

R L L F R L L F L
[4] [4] [1] [4] [4] [1] [4] [4] [1] [4] [1]

Sixteenth-Note Fill 4.5 (4- and 1-note groupings | Combination 4)

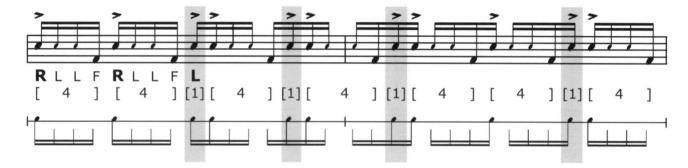

R L L F R L L F L
[4] [4] [1] [4] [1] [4] [1] [4] [4] [1] [4]

The Principle

Play the *4-note groupings using sixteenth notes*. By combining it with the *1-note grouping* you will play the 4-note grouping in all four positions.

Subdivision of fills: **Sixteenth notes**
Grid of underlying rhythm: **Sixteenth notes**

Photo © Marco Hammer

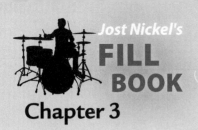
Fills Using Eighth-Note Triplets

Fills Using Eighth-Note Triplets 1 (2- and 3-Note Groupings)

In this chapter, we will explore different ways of playing fills using *eighth-note triplets*.

Practice Tip

As the fills are now based on eighth-note triplets, your grooves should be as well. Combine the following fills with a shuffle groove, and count the quarter-note pulse out loud, especially during the fills.

Let's begin with the well-known 2- and 3-note groupings. First, the *2-note grouping*.

2-Note Grouping (Original figure R L)

R   L

Now play the 2-note grouping over *one bar*, where you must pay attention to the accent! You will see the underlying rhythm for each fill in *line 2*.

Eighth-Note Triplet Fill 1.1 (2-note grouping over one bar | Position 1)    CD 15

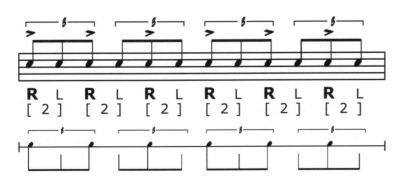

6 Over 4 Polyrhythms:

When you play the 2-note grouping using eighth-note triplets and accent the right hand, you will hear exactly six accents in a bar of $\frac{4}{4}$ time.

The underlying rhythmic principle of this fill is called either a **6 over 4** polyrhythm, because you distribute six accents evenly over a $\frac{4}{4}$ time, or **quarter-note triplets**.

As I have always written down the underlying rhythm for the sake of simplicity with all the relevant subdivisions, you don't actually see quarter-note triplets in the notation for the *2-note grouping* (*original figure on page 47*). So, here's the underlying rhythm notated with all subdivisions in *line 1* and quarter-note triplets in *line 2*. Rhythmically, both are the same!

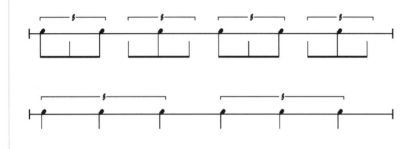

Now displace the 2-note grouping by *one beat* to the right. The fill is also based on the **6 over 4 principle**, except that now you'll begin on the *second beat* of the eighth-note triplet. The *right hand* continues to play the accents.

Eighth-Note Triplet Fill 1.2 (2-note grouping over one bar | Position 2)

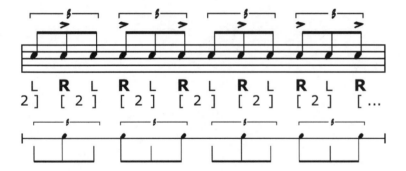

Now that you've played both positions of the 2-note grouping, let's take a look at *3-note groupings* using eighth-note triplets.

Eighth-Note Triplet Fill 1.3 (Original figure)

Before you combine the 3-note grouping with the 2-note grouping, you should practice the *three* possible positions of the 3-note grouping:

Eighth-Note Triplet Fill 1.4 (3-note grouping over one bar | Position 1)

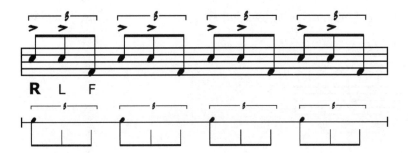

Now displace the 3-note grouping by *one beat* of the eighth-note triplet to the right. Play the *right hand* on the *second* eighth note of the triplet. The sticking remains as **R L F**.

Eighth-Note Triplet Fill 1.5 (3-note grouping over one bar | Position 2)

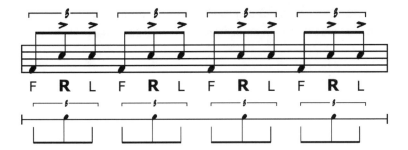

Practice Tip

I always think of the 3-note grouping in the order of **R L F**. Even if—as in *Eighth-Note Triplet Fill 1.5*—the bass drum plays on beat 1, the order for me is still **R L F**, starting on the *second beat* of the eighth-note triplet. My way of thinking about groups of any kind remains the same, regardless of their position in the bar.

Last but not least, the third position: the right hand plays on the *third* eighth note of the triplet.

Eighth-Note Triplet Fill 1.6 (3-note grouping over one bar | Position 3)

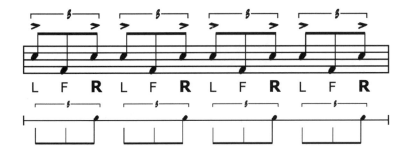

Now combine the 2- and 3-note groupings within *one-bar fills*.

Eighth-Note Triplet Fill 1.7 (2- and 3-note groupings | Combination 1)

CD 16

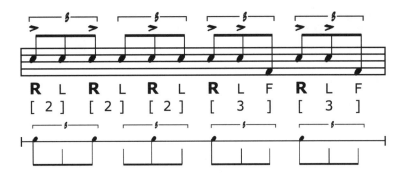

Also, in the case of triplet fills, it is really important to listen to the fundamental (eighth-note triplet) rhythm.

Here are two ways in which you can clarify the rhythm using *Eighth-Note Triplet Fill 1.7*:

1. Play the fill in **bar 1**, and in **bar 2**, play the rhythm on the snare drum. To do this, play eighth-note triplets with singles, and emphasize the rhythm. At the same time, play the quarter-note pulse with the pedaled hi-hat to further enhance your understanding.

2. Play the fill in **bar 1**, and in **bar 2**, play a groove with the underlying rhythm as a bass-drum figure.

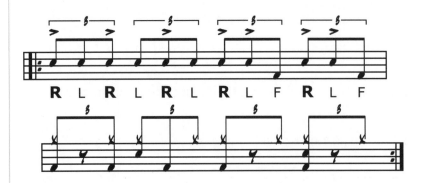

Here are further combinations of the 2- and 3-note groupings.

Eighth-Note Triplet Fill 1.8 (2- and 3-note groupings | Combination 2)

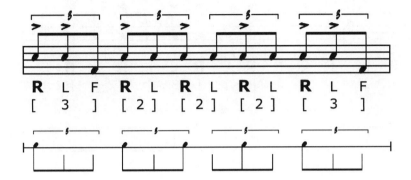

Eighth-Note Triplet Fill 1.9 (2- and 3-note groupings | Combination 3)

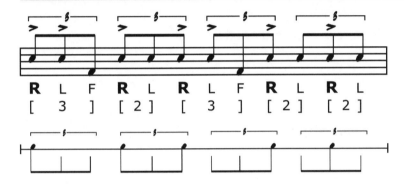

Eighth-Note Triplet Fill 1.10 (2- and 3-note groupings | Combination 4)

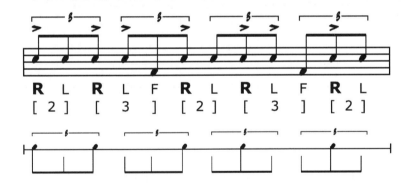

In the following two-bar combination examples, the 2-note groupings are marked in gray.

Eighth-Note Triplet Fill 1.11 (Two bars | Combination 1)

CD 17

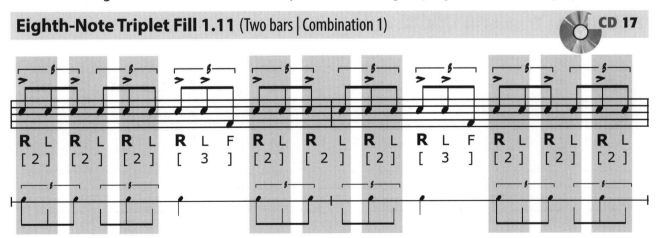

Eighth-Note Triplet Fill 1.12 (Two bars | Combination 2)

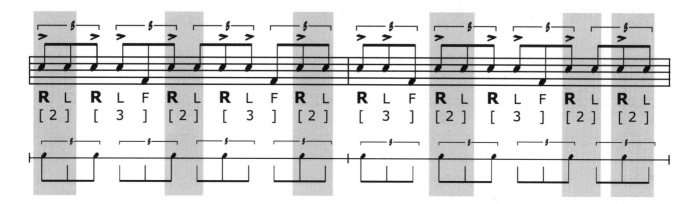

Play both of the following fills just using the numbers (in *square brackets* below the notation) so you can gradually get rid of the notes.

I've left out the sticking, but the notes are still there in case you need a visual:

[2] = R L

[3] = R L F

Eighth-Note Triplet Fill 1.13 (Two bars | Combination 3)

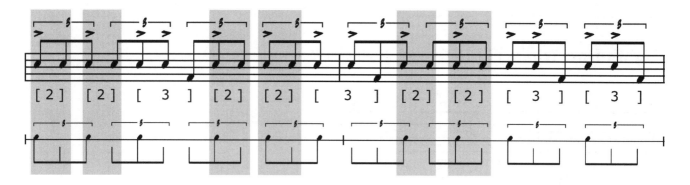

The "+1" in the following *Eighth-Note Triplet Fill 1.14* means that one beat is missing until both bars are complete. Play the last beat with the *left hand*. Then play beat 1 with the *right hand* after the fill.

Eighth-Note Triplet Fill 1.14 (Two bars | Combination 4)

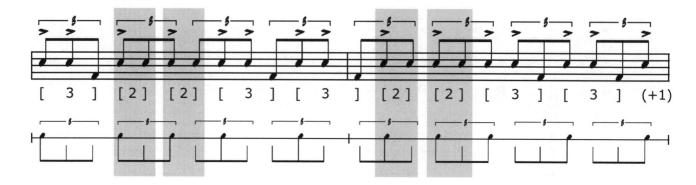

Now practice additional combinations so you become absolutely comfortable playing 3- and 2-note groupings. You know the motifs, you know the principle. It is now only about practicing different combinations. To do this, you need to work with place holders (the numbers 3 and 2). The following four combinations of 3- and 2-note groupings each represent a *two-bar fill* in $\frac{4}{4}$ time. You can see the counting in the *second line*, so you know where you are.

Eighth-Note Triplet Fill 1.15 (Two bars | Combination 5)

Eighth-Note Triplet Fill 1.16 (Two bars | Combination 6)

In the following *Eighth-Note Triplet Fill 1.17*, you will see "+1" at the end. Play with the *left hand* here.

Eighth-Note Triplet Fill 1.17 (Two bars | Combination 7)

3			2	3		2	2	3	2	3		3			+1
1	+	a	2	+	a	3	+	a	4	+	a	1	+	a
2	+	a	3	+	a	4	+	a

Eighth-Note Triplet Fill 1.18 (Two bars | Combination 8)

2	3		3		2	3		3		2	3		3		
1	+	a	2	+	a	3	+	a	4	+	a	1	+	a	2	+	a	3	+	a	4	+	a

The Principle

Play *3- and 2-note groupings using eighth-note triplets*. By combining them with the 2-note grouping, you will play the 3-note grouping in all *three* positions.

Subdivision of fills: **Eighth-note triplets**
Grid of underlying rhythm: **Eighth-note triplets**

Fills Using Eighth-Note Triplets 2 (4- and 3-Note Groupings)

On the topic of triplets, there are *two polyrhythms* you should definitely know about.
You already know the first polyrhythm: **6 over 4** (*see page 48*).

The *second* polyrhythm is created when you play a 4-note grouping using triplets. We'll use the *4-note grouping* you already know:

4-Note Grouping (Original figure)

Make sure you play both unaccented notes quietly in the *left hand*.
The bass-drum beat at the end should be about as loud as the accent at the beginning.

Now play the 4-note grouping over *one* bar. You can see the underlying rhythm in *line 2*.

Eighth-Note Triplet Fill 2.1 (4-note grouping over one bar | Position 1) **CD 19**

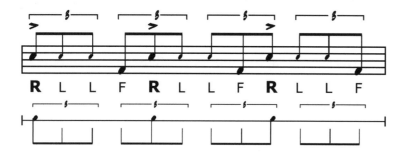

3 over 4 Polyrhythm:

When playing the 4-note grouping using eighth-note triplets, you have exactly *three* accents in one bar of $\frac{4}{4}$ time.

The fundamental rhythmic principle of this fill is called either a **3 over 4 polyrhythm**, because you distribute three accents evenly over $\frac{4}{4}$ time, or a *half-note triplet*.

Because I've always written down the underlying rhythm with all relevant subdivisions for the sake of simplicity, you don't actually see half-note triplets in the notation.

So, here's the underlying rhythm notated with all subdivisions in *line 1* and half-note triplets in *line 2*. Rhythmically, both are the same!

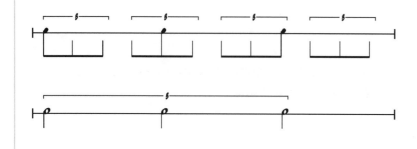

In a 4-note grouping there are—the name gives it away—four different positions.

Here is *Position 2*. The 4-note grouping is displaced by *one* beat of the eighth-note triplet further to the right.

Eighth-Note Triplet Fill 2.2 (4-note grouping over one bar | Position 2)

... and *another* beat of the eighth-note triplet further to the right ...

Eighth-Note Triplet Fill 2.3 (4-note grouping over one bar | Position 3)

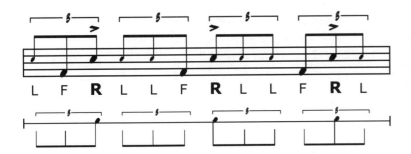

You'll see the fourth and final position below in *Eighth-Note Triplet Fill 2.4*.

Eighth-Note Triplet Fill 2.4 (4-note grouping over one bar | Position 4)

Now combine the 4-note grouping with the 3-note grouping.

We've already covered the 3-note grouping—use the sticking **R L F**.

Both hands are accented.

3-Note Grouping (Original figure)

All positions of the 3-note grouping occur within the following *three-bar exercise.* The 4-note groupings are marked in **gray**. You'll see the basic rhythmic structure in the *second line*.

Eighth-Note Triplet Fill 2.5 (Exercise over 3 bars)

This is followed by eight, two-bar combinations of 3- and 4-note groupings.

Eighth-Note Triplet Fill 2.6 (4- and 3-note groupings | Combination 1)   **CD 20**

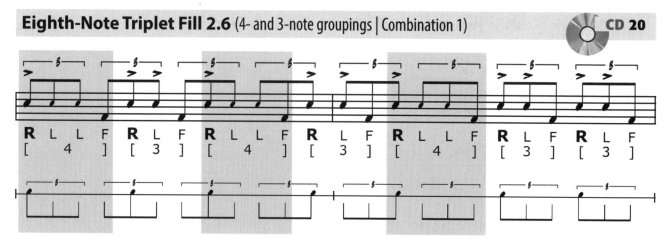

Eighth-Note Triplet Fill 2.7 (4- and 3-note groupings | Combination 2)

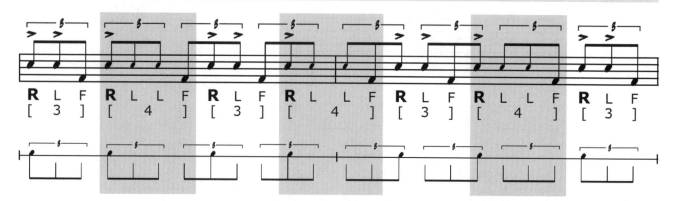

Cross-Reference

In the *Appendix, on page 134,* you will find a snare-drum exercise in which the 4- and 3-note groupings are combined. The aim of this is to further the basic rhythmic idea.
It is useful to practice snare-drum exercises and fills during the same practice session.

Play both of the following fills by just using the numbers (in *square brackets* below the notation) so you can gradually get rid of the notes.

I've left out the sticking, but the notes appear below in case you need a visual.

[4] = R L L F

[3] = R L F

Eighth-Note Triplet Fill 2.8 (4- and 3-note groupings | Combination 3)

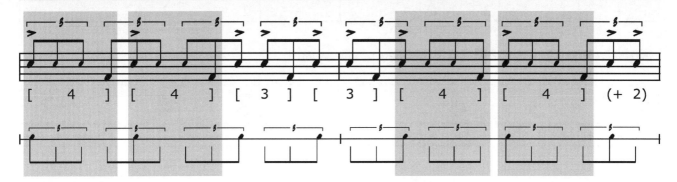

Eighth-Note Triplet Fill 2.9 (4- and 3-note groupings | Combination 4)

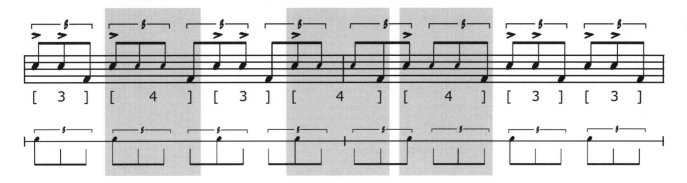

Now practice additional combinations so you become absolutely comfortable when dealing with 4- and 3-note groupings. Because you already know the motifs, it is now only about practicing different combinations. To do this, you need to work with place holders (the numbers 4 and 3). The following four combinations of 4- and 3-note groupings each represent a *two-bar fill* in $\frac{4}{4}$ time. As always, in the *second line*, you can see the counting so you know where you are.

Eighth-Note Triplet Fill 2.10 (Two bars | Combination 5)

3	4		3	3		4		3	4	
1	+	a	2	+	a	3	+	a	4	+	a	1	+	a	2	+	a	3	+	a	4	+	a

Eighth-Note Triplet Fill 2.11 (Two bars | Combination 6)

3	3		4		3	3		4		4		
1	+	a	2	+	a	3	+	a	4	+	a	1	+	a	2	+	a	3	+	a	4	+	a

In the following examples, *Eighth-Note Triplet Fills 2.12* and *2.13*, you will see "+2" at the end. This means another two beats are missing until two bars are complete. Here you simply play **R L** (two eighth-note triplets).

Eighth-Note Triplet Fill 2.12 (Two bars | Combination 7)

3	4		4		4		3	4		+2

1	+	a	2	+	a	3	+	a	4	+	a	1	+	a	2	+	a	3	+	a	4	+	a

Eighth-Note Triplet Fill 2.13 (Two bars | Combination 8)

4	3		4		4		3	4		+2

1	+	a	2	+	a	3	+	a	4	+	a	1	+	a	2	+	a	3	+	a	4	+	a

Orchestration Tip

Bring the toms into play by playing the 3-note grouping with the *right hand* on the floor tom, and the *left hand* on the rack tom. The orchestration of the 4-note grouping remains unchanged.

The Principle

Play *4- and 3-note groupings using eighth-note triplets*. Through these combinations, you will play both groups in all positions.

Subdivision of fills: **Eighth-note triplets**
Grid of underlying rhythm: **Eighth-note triplets**

And so it continues:

Now practice all the two-bar combinations using the instructions below.

This is best done with **Reading Text 3** (*4- and 3-Note Groupings Using Eighth-Note Triplets*). There you will find an overview of all the combinations (*examples 2.6–2.13*).

Practice Steps	
Start tempo	Quarter note = 91
Number of tempos	4
Number of rounds per tempo	Every fill of the reading text 2 times
Musical form	2-bar groove + 2-bar fill
Count out loud	Quarter note and "click"	eighth-note triplets when required
Duration of exercise	Around 15 minutes

This rhythmic concept (*4- and 3-note groupings*) can be easily transferred to other motifs.

For example:

Play the 4-note grouping with two bass-drum beats (we've already done this with the 4-note grouping using sixteenth notes on *page 42*). The 3-note grouping remains the same.

"Two Bass-Drum Beats" 1 (Original figure)

4-note grouping

R   L   F   F

3-note grouping

R   L   F

Now combine the 4- and 3-note groupings with the help of **Reading Text 3** (*4- and 3-Note Groupings Using Eighth-Note Triplets*). Here's *Combination 1* of the reading text to be used as the basis for the following fill.

4			3			4			3			4			3			3		
1	+	a	2	+	a	3	+	a	4	+	a	1	+	a	2	+	a	3	+	a	4	+	a

"Two Bass-Drum Beats" 2 (Combination 1 from Reading Text 3)

CD 22

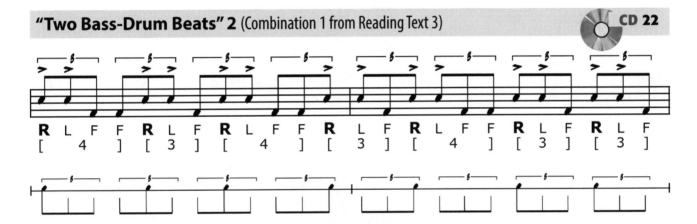

During practice, play the other combinations of **Reading Text 3** using the toms instead of the snare.

Practice Steps	
Start tempo	Quarter note = 91
Number of tempos	4
Number of rounds per tempo	Every fill of the reading text 2 times
Musical form	2-bar groove + 2-bar fill
Count out loud	Quarter note and "click" | eighth-note triplets when required
Duration of exercise	Around 15 minutes

The orchestration concept, *switch orchestration*, presented in *Chapter 1* on *pages 13 and 14*, can be wonderfully transferred to the 4- and 3-note groupings, as the hands play single strokes here.

To recap:
Switch Orchestration only uses three instruments.
Normal orchestration:
Right hand: floor tom
Left hand: hi-hat
Foot: bass drum

Then the following happens:
The right and left hands switch instruments.

Switch orchestration:
Right hand: hi-hat
Left hand: floor tom
Foot: bass drum

Now do the *switch* as follows:

Play *two times* through the "normal" variation followed by *one* switch, and then repeat again from the beginning until the fill has ended (play every third group as a switch).

"Two Bass-Drum Beats" 3 (Combination 1 from Reading Text 3 | Switch)   www.jostnickel.com

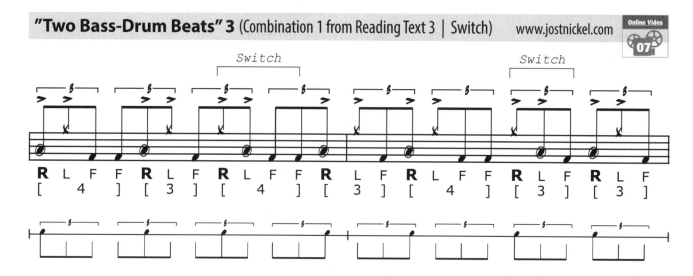

In my opinion, it is not necessary to play all combinations with the *switch orchestration*. It is enough if you only apply the principle to one or two combinations.

The book continues here with *sixteenth-note triplet fills*.

Photo © Arnd Geise

Fills Using Sixteenth-Note Triplets

In this chapter, I'll show you some different ways to play fills using *sixteenth-note triplets*.

Fills Using Sixteenth-Note Triplets 1 (6- and 3-Note Groupings)

As you did at the beginning of *Chapter 2*, play a figure that is exactly *one quarter note* long. In sixteenth-note triplets, this equals six beats.

Sixteenth-Note Triplet Fill 1 (Original figure: R L R L L F)

Sixteenth-Note Triplet Fill 1.1 (Original figure over one bar | 6-note grouping)

 CD 23

The original figure will be called a *6-note grouping* from now on.

Tip for Dynamics

Make sure you play both of the unaccented notes in the left hand quietly.
The bass-drum beat at the end should be about as loud as the three accents at the beginning.

Next we are going to displace the 6-note grouping by one eighth note from the downbeat to the offbeat. That means the 6-note grouping now begins on the eighth-note offbeat (on beat 1+), and sounds completely different in relation to the quarter-note pulse.

Play a snare-drum accent on beat 1 and then the 6-note grouping starting on beat 1+.

Sixteenth-Note Triplet Fill 1.2 (6-note grouping displaced by one eighth note)

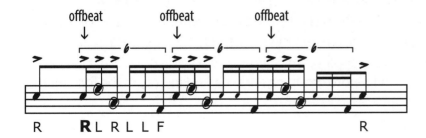

Now let's add *Sixteenth-Note Triplet Fills 1.1* and *1.2* together to create a *two-bar fill*.

Although the subdivision of the fills is sixteenth-note triplets, the underlying rhythm is eighth notes. For clarification look at the rhythmic structure of the fill in *line 2*.

Sixteenth-Note Triplet Fill 1.3 (Combination of Sixteenth-Note Triplet Fills 1.1 and 1.2)

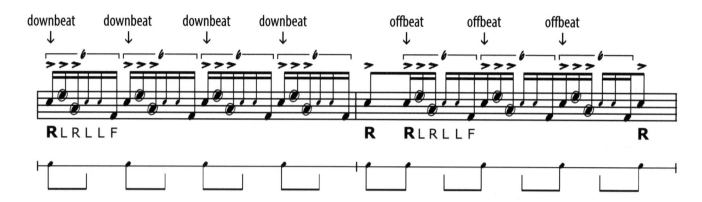

Tip

Eighth notes are the underlying rhythm of the 6- and 3-note groupings using sixteenth-note triplets. *Chapter 2 (page 31)* describes how you can make the underlying rhythm clear for yourself.

Next, play a better transition between the two positions of the original figure. Instead of playing the eighth note on the snare drum (*see Sixteenth-Note Triplet Fill 1.3*, bar 2, beats 1 and 4+), play the following three beats using sixteenth-note triplets, which together are exactly one eighth note long.

Sixteenth-Note Triplet Fill 1.4 (R L F)

Sixteenth-Note Triplet Fill 1.4 is three sixteenth-note triplets long and is our *3-note grouping*.

Now add the 3-note grouping to the *two-bar fill*, which you learned in *Sixteenth-Note Triplet Fill 1.3*.

Start the fill with the 6-note grouping on beat 1 (*downbeat*). On beat 1 of bar 2, play the 3-note grouping *once*, directly followed by the 6-note grouping, which you now play on the offbeat (1+). To finish, play the 3-note grouping on beat 4+. All 3-note groupings are marked in **gray** in the following fill.

Sixteenth-Note Triplet Fill 1.5 (6- and 3-note groupings | Combination 1)

CD 24

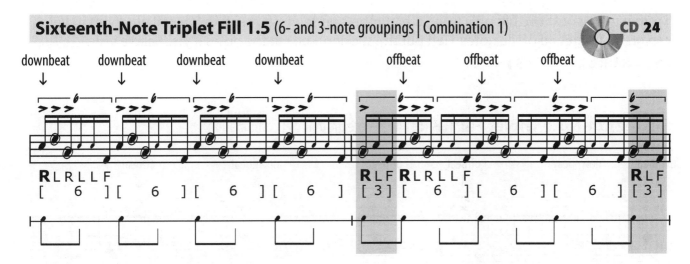

Now alternate between playing the 6-note grouping and the 3-note grouping (marked in **gray**). In this way, the position of the 6-note grouping always changes from downbeat to offbeat and back again.

Sixteenth-Note Triplet Fill 1.6 (6- and 3-note groupings | Combination 2)

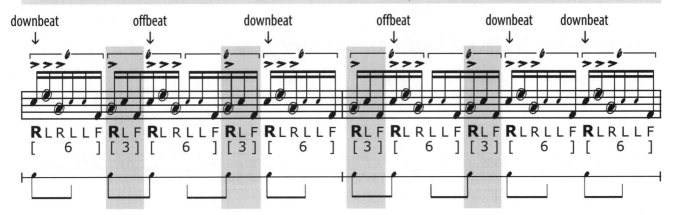

Sixteenth-Note Triplet Fill 1.7 shows another way of combining the 6-note grouping with the 3-note grouping (marked in **gray**). Start here with the 3-note grouping, which means the first 6-note grouping begins on the offbeat.

Sixteenth-Note Triplet Fill 1.7 (6- and 3-note groupings | Combination 3)

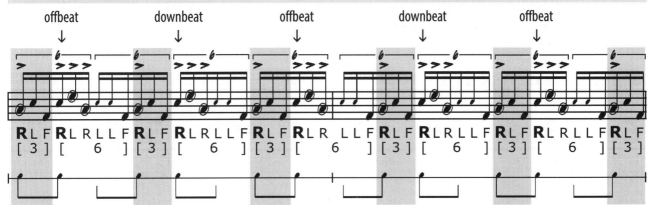

Cross-Reference

On the topic of 6- and 3-note groupings, you'll find a snare exercise in the *Appendix* (*see page 135*). The aim of the snare exercise is to further the basic rhythmic idea. It is useful to practice snare-drum exercises and fills during the same practice session.

Try to play the next two fills only using the numbers (in *square brackets* below the notation) so you can gradually get rid of the notes. I left out the sticking. Look at the notes if you need a visual.

[6] = R L R L L F   [3] = R L F

Sixteenth-Note Triplet Fill 1.8 (6- and 3-note groupings | Combination 4)

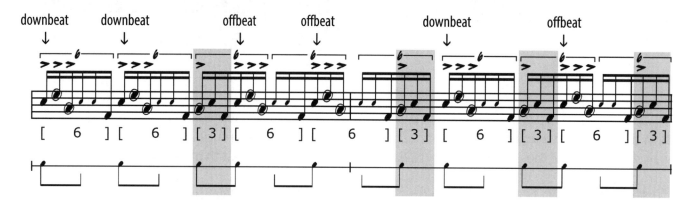

Sixteenth-Note Triplet Fill 1.9 (6- and 3-note groupings | Combination 5)

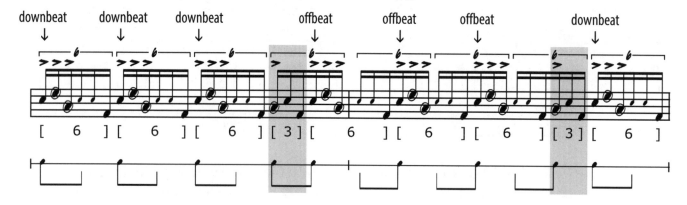

To become rhythmically confident when dealing with the 6- and 3-note groupings, you can practice more combinations by working with place holders (the numbers 6 and 3). The following four combinations of 6- and 3-note groupings each represent one *two-bar fill* in $\frac{4}{4}$ time.

Sixteenth-Note Triplet Fill 1.10 (6- and 3-note groupings | Combination 6)   CD 25

6		3	6		6		3	6		6		3	6		3	
1	+	2	+	3	+	4	+	1	+	2	+	3	+	4	+

Sixteenth-Note Triplet Fill 1.11 (6- and 3-note groupings | Combination 7)

3	6		6		6		3	6		6		3	6		3	
1	+	2	+	3	+	4	+	1	+	2	+	3	+	4	+

Sixteenth-Note Triplet Fill 1.12 (6- and 3-note groupings | Combination 8)

3	6		3	3	6		3	6		3	6		6		3
1	+	2	+	3	+	4	+	1	+	2	+	3	+	4	+

Sixteenth-Note Triplet Fill 1.13 (6- and 3-note groupings | Combination 9)

6		6		3	3	3	6		3	3	6		3	6	
1	+	2	+	3	+	4	+	1	+	2	+	3	+	4	+

The Principle

Play the *6-note grouping using sixteenth-note triplets*. In combination with the *3-note grouping*, the *6-note grouping* always changes between the downbeat and the offbeat.

Subdivision of fills: **Sixteenth-note triplets**

Grid of underlying rhythm: **Eighth notes**

Now practice all the two-bar combinations using the instructions below.

This is best done with **Reading Text 4** (*6- and 3-Note Groupings Using Sixteenth-Note Triplets*). There you will find an overview of all combinations (*examples 1.5–1.13*).

Practice Steps	
Start tempo	Quarter note = 60
Number of tempos	3
Number of rounds per tempo	Every fill of the reading text 2 times
Musical form	2-bar groove + 2-bar fill
Count out loud	Quarter note and "click"	eighth notes when required
Duration of exercise	Around 15 minutes

Transfer the rhythmic concept to other motifs as in the following example.

For example:

The *6-note grouping* now consists of four accented single strokes with the hands, followed by two bass-drum beats at the end of the figure. The left hand stays on the rack tom, and the right hand changes between the snare drum and floor tom.

In the *3-note grouping*, the right hand plays an accent on the floor tom, followed by two ghost notes with the left hand on the snare drum.

The contrast between the many accents of the 6-note grouping and the ghost notes in the 3-note grouping make the fill sound very varied.

"Two Bass-Drum Beats" 1 (Original figure)

6-note grouping

R L R L F F

3-note grouping

R L L

Now combine the *6- and 3-note groupings* with help from **Reading Text 4** (*6- and 3-Note Groupings Using Sixteenth-Note Triplets*). *Combination 1* of this reading text is the basis for the following fill.

6		6		6		6		3	6		6		6		3
1	+	2	+	3	+	4	+	1	+	2	+	3	+	4	+

"Two Bass-Drum Beats" 2 (Combination 1 from Reading Text 4)

CD 26

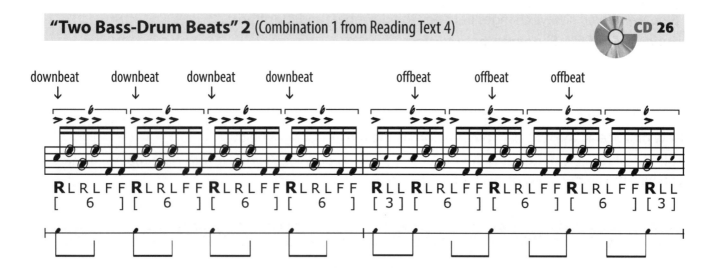

Practice Steps	
Start tempo	Quarter note = 60
Number of tempos	3
Number of rounds per tempo	Every fill of the reading text 2 times
Musical form	2-bar groove + 2-bar fill
Count out loud	Quarter note and "click" | eighth notes when required
Duration of exercise	Around 15 minutes

Think of your own combinations!

Next, we will cover *9-note groupings* using sixteenth-note triplets.

Fills Using Sixteenth-Note Triplets 2 (9-Note Groupings)

9-note groupings using sixteenth-note triplets are very popular with a lot of drummers. As the name suggests, the next fill is *nine* sixteenth-note triplets long.

Sixteenth-Note Triplet Fill 2 (9-note grouping | original figure 1)

R L L F R L R L F

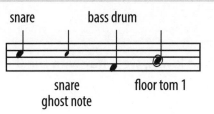

Repeat the original figure often enough that it creates a *two-bar fill*. Because the original figure is nine sixteenth-note triplets long, it automatically changes between the downbeat and the offbeat.

In *line 2*, you can see the underlying rhythm of the fills, which still consists of eighth notes. Every second round is marked in **gray**.

Sixteenth-Note Triplet Fill 2.1 (9-note grouping | original figure 1 over two bars)

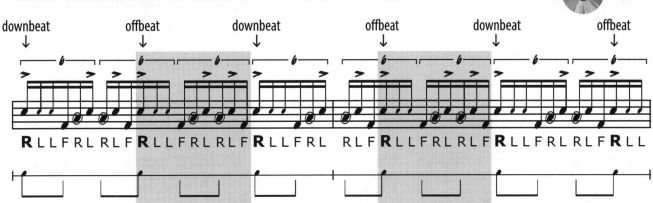

To increase your flexibility in dealing with this figure, practice starting the 9-note grouping on every eighth note in the bar.

In the next example, the 9-note grouping begins on beat 1+.

Sixteenth-Note triplet Fill 2.2 (9-note grouping | original figure 1 starting on beat 1+)

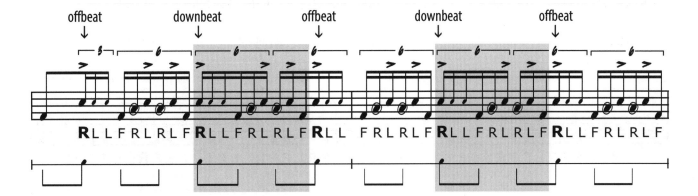

The Principle

Play the *9-note grouping* using sixteenth-note triplets. Because the 9-note groupings are exactly *three* eighth notes long, they always change back and forth between the downbeat and the offbeat.

Subdivision of fills: **Sixteenth-note triplets**

Grid of underlying rhythm: **Eighth notes**

As it's so lovely, we'll stay with the 9-note grouping. Here is another figure with lots of bass-drum beats.

Sixteenth-Note Triplet Fill 2.3 (9-note grouping | original figure 2)

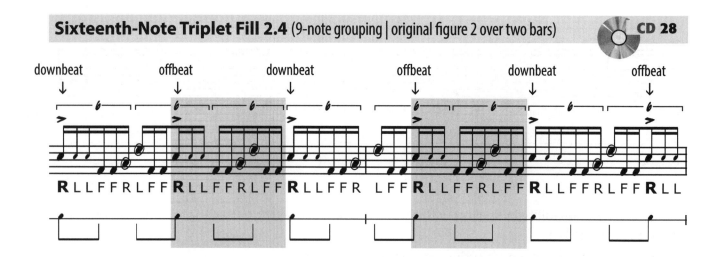

After learning the original figure, play it again over two bars. Every second round is marked in **gray**.

Sixteenth-Note Triplet Fill 2.4 (9-note grouping | original figure 2 over two bars)   **CD 28**

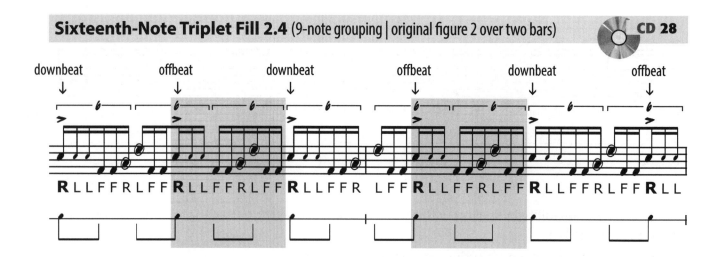

In the following example, this 9-note grouping also starts on beat 1+.

Sixteenth-Note Triplet Fill 2.5 (9-note grouping | original figure 2 starting on beat 1+)

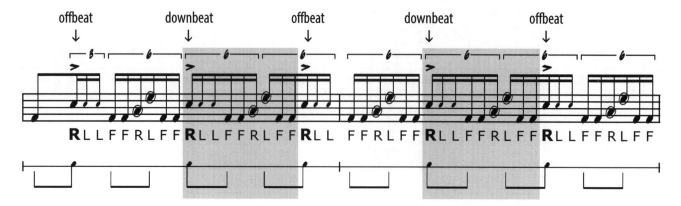

To make an easy transition back to the groove after the fill on the previous page, replace the last two bass-drum beats with the hands (**R L**). Now you can comfortably play a bass drum on beat 1 of your grooves.

Next is one of my favorite 9-note groupings, which is completely without toms. You can play this figure very nicely in a jazz context.

Sixteenth-Note Triplet Fill 2.6 (9-note grouping | original figure 3)

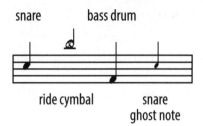

You should also play this figure over two bars.

Sixteenth-Note Triplet Fill 2.7 (9-note grouping | original figure 3 over two bars)   CD 29

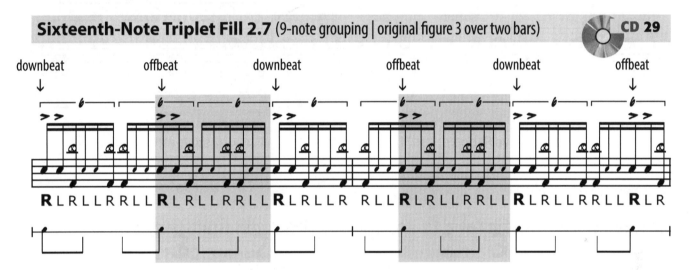

In order to make a smooth transition back to the groove possible after the above fill, I only play the bass drum (without the ride cymbal) on the last beat of the above fill.

And now—you guessed it—the 9-note grouping begins on beat 1+.

Sixteenth-Note Triplet Fill 2.8 (9-note grouping | original figure 3 starting on beat 1+)

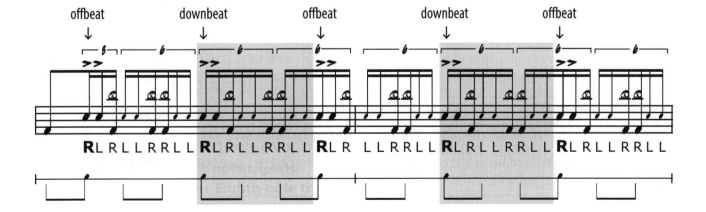

Here is the fourth and last 9-note grouping.

Sixteenth-Note Triplet Fill 2.9 (9-note grouping | original figure 4)

F F L R R L R L L

The procedure stays the same. First play the figure over two bars:

Sixteenth-Note Triplet Fill 2.10 (9-note grouping | original figure 4 over two bars)   CD 30

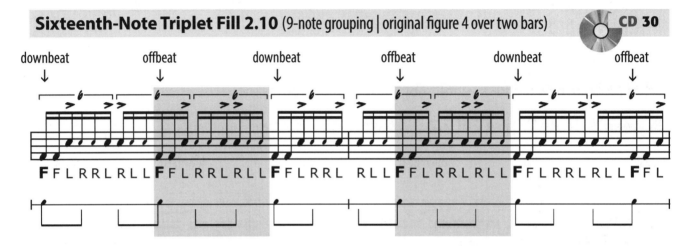

And then start on beat 1+.

Sixteenth-Note Triplet Fill 2.11 (9-note grouping | original figure 4 starting on beat 1+)

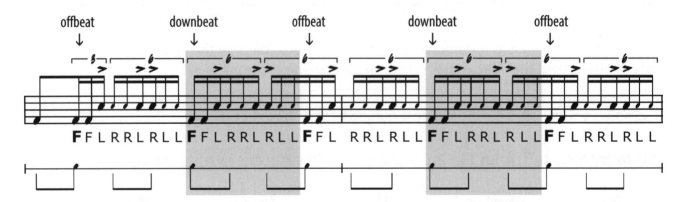

The 9-note groupings above are some of my favorites. You can find every single one in my playing. But the rhythmic principle is much more important than the exact motifs. Through the use of 9-note groupings using sixteenth-note triplets, the fill wanders automatically back and forth between the downbeat and the offbeat. So if you think, *"I'd like to have a fill I can use with my double pedal,"* then simply think of one that has nine beats, and you can start immediately.

The underlying rhythm of both fill concepts in this chapter is based on straight eighth notes. We're now coming to a different idea.

Fills Using Sixteenth-Note Triplets 3 (4- and 6-Note Groupings)

From this point on the underlying rhythm of the fills changes from eighth notes to eighth-note triplets. The subdivision of the fill itself remains unchanged, which means you still play fills using sixteenth-note triplets.

First is a new figure that is four beats long (*4-note grouping*).

Sixteenth-Note Triplet Fill 3 (Original figure)

Practice Tip

As the fills are now based on eighth-note triplets, your grooves should be as well. Combine the following fills with a shuffle groove and, in particular, count the quarter-note pulse out loud during the fills.

Now play a shuffle groove over three bars and then the original figure as a *one-bar fill* using sixteenth-note triplets. You'll see the underlying rhythm in *line 2*.

Sixteenth-Note Triplet Fill 3.1 (Original figure over one bar)

CD 31

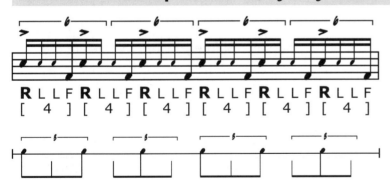

The underlying rhythmic principle of this fill is quarter-note triplets e.g., the **6 over 4** (*see the explanation on page 48*). Play six evenly distributed snare-drum accents in a bar of $\frac{4}{4}$ time.

Tip

The underlying rhythm here is based on eighth-note triplets.

Chapter 3 (page 50) describes how you can make the underlying rhythm clear to yourself.

The following fill is also based on the **6 over 4** principle, except you now start the fill on the *second beat* of the eighth-note triplet.

Sixteenth-Note Triplet Fill 3.2 (Original figure over one bar | starting on the 2nd beat of the eighth-note triplet)

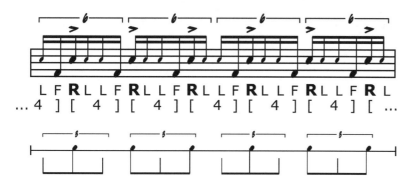

Here is a version of the above fills that is more playable with a different lead-in and an extra accent at the end (both marked in **gray**).

Sixteenth-Note Triplet Fill 3.3 (Original figure over one bar | starting on the 2nd beat of the eighth-note triplet)

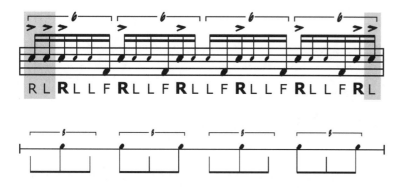

The headline of this chapter talks about 4- and 6-note groupings. Before you ask, "Where are the *6-note groupings?*" here they are.

Here is the previously covered 6-note grouping.

Sixteenth-Note Triplet Fill 3.4 (6-note grouping)

You have already played the 6-note grouping, but the fill sounds very different in a triplet context. The following two-bar exercise will help you understand exactly what the *right hand* plays. Alternate between just playing the right hand and then the whole fill.

Sixteenth-Note Triplet Fill 3.5 (6-note grouping over one bar with preliminary exercise)

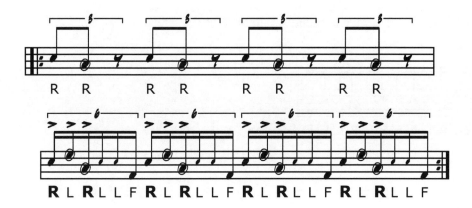

Now displace the 6-note grouping written above by one eighth-note triplet. It now begins on the *third beat* of the eighth-note triplet.

Sixteenth-Note Triplet Fill 3.5A (6-note grouping | Position 2 with preliminary exercise)

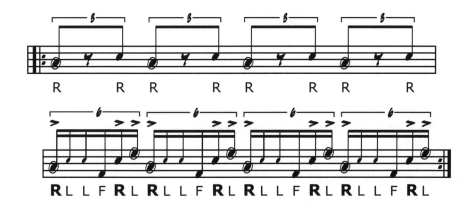

Here is the third and last position of the 6-note grouping, beginning on the *second beat* of the eighth-note triplet.

Sixteenth-Note Triplet Fill 3.5B (6-note grouping | Position 3 with preliminary exercise)

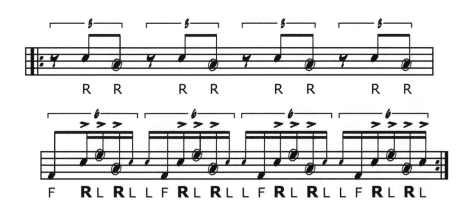

Now combine the 4- and 6-note groupings into *one-bar fills*. You will see the underlying rhythm in *line 2*. Always play *three* bars of shuffle groove, followed by a *one-bar fill*.

 CD 32

Sixteenth-Note Triplet Fill 3.6 (4- and 6-note groupings | Combination 1)

Sixteenth-Note Triplet Fill 3.7 (4- and 6-note groupings | Combination 2)

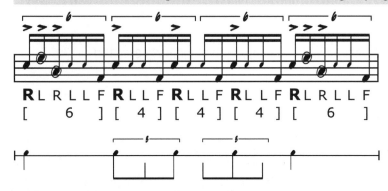

Sixteenth-Note Triplet Fill 3.8 (4- and 6-note groupings | Combination 3)

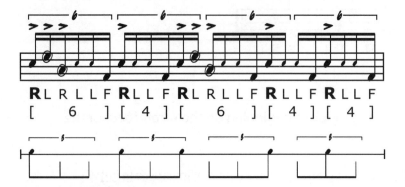

Sixteenth-Note Triplet Fill 3.9 (4- and 6-note groupings | Combination 4)

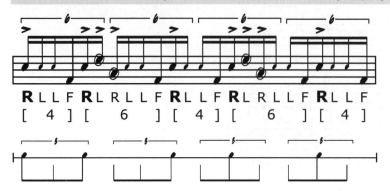

In the following two-bar combinations, the 4-note groupings are marked in **gray**.

Now play *two bars* of a shuffle groove and *two bars* of fill.

Sixteenth-Note Triplet Fill **3.10** (Two bars | Combination 1)

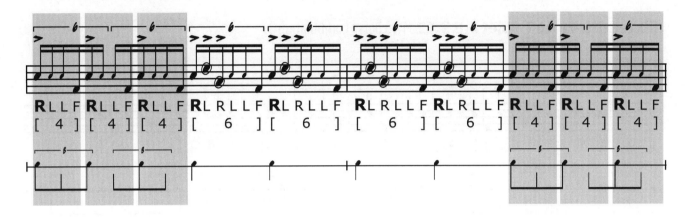

Sixteenth-Note Triplet Fill **3.11** (Two bars | Combination 2) CD 33

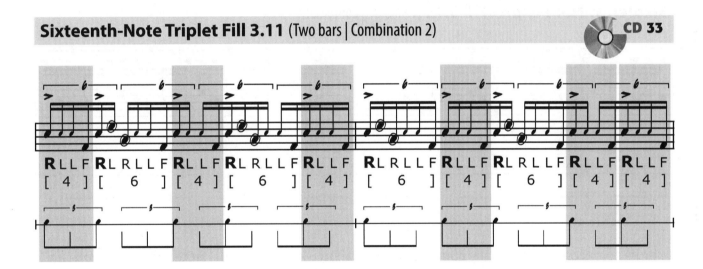

Cross-Reference

On the topic of 6- and 4-note groupings, there is a snare-drum exercise in the *Appendix* (*see page 137*). The goal here is to also further the basic rhythmic idea. It is useful to practice snare-drum exercises and fills during the same practice session.

Play both of the following fills using the numbers (in *square brackets* below the notation) to help memorize them.

[6] = R L R L L F
[4] = R L L F

Sixteenth-Note Triplet Fill 3.12 (Two bars | Combination 3)

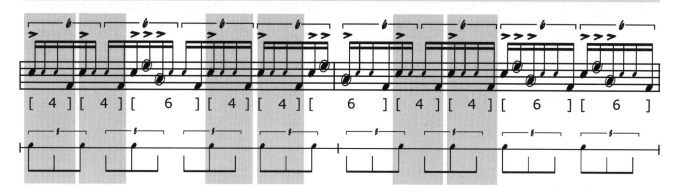

Sixteenth-Note Triplet Fill 3.13 (Two bars | Combination 4)

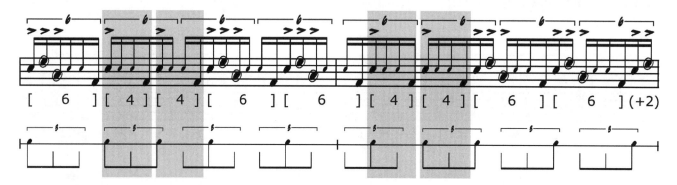

In order to become rhythmically comfortable in dealing with the 6- and 4-note groupings, you can practice other combinations according to the principle. For this, you can work with place holders (the numbers 6 and 4). The following four combinations of 6- and 4-note groupings each represent one *two-bar fill* in $\frac{4}{4}$ time.

Sixteenth-Note Triplet Fill 3.14 (Two bars | Combination 5)   CD 34

4	6		4	4	6		4	6		6		4	4
1	+	a	2	+	a	3	+	a	4	+	a	1	+	a	2	+	a	3	+	a	4	+	a

Sixteenth-Note Triplet Fill 3.15 (Two bars | Combination 6)

4	4	6		4	6		6		4	6		4	4
1	+	a	2	+	a	3	+	a	4	+	a	1	+	a	2	+	a	3	+	a	4	+	a

In the following *Sixteenth-Note Triplet Fill 3.16*, you'll see "+2" at the end. This means two beats are missing until the bar is complete. You simply play **R L** here (two sixteenth-note triplets).

Sixteenth-Note Triplet Fill 3.16 (Two bars | Combination 7)

6	4	6		4	4	6		4	6		6		+2
1	+	a	2	+	a	3	+	a	4	+	a	1	+	a	2	+	a	3	+	a	4	+	a

Sixteenth-Note Triplet Fill 3.17 (Two bars | Combination 8)

4	6		6		4	6		6		4	6		6	
1	+	a	2	+	a	3	+	a	4	+	a	1	+	a	2	+	a	3	+	a	4	+	a

The Principle

Play *6- and 4-note groupings using sixteenth-note triplets*. The combination results in fills that are based on eighth-note triplets.

Subdivision of fills: **Sixteenth-note triplets**

Grid of underlying rhythm: **Eighth-note triplets**

Now practice all the two-bar combinations using the instructions below.

This is best done with **Reading Text 5** (*6- and 4-Note Groupings Using Sixteenth-Note Triplets*). There you will find an overview of all combinations (*examples 3.10–3.17*).

Practice Steps	
Start tempo	Quarter note = 60
Number of tempos	3
Number of rounds per tempo	Every fill of the reading text 2 times
Musical form	2-bar groove + 2-bar fill
Count out loud	Quarter note and "click"	eighth-note triplets when required
Duration of exercise	Around 15 minutes

Now transfer this rhythmic concept to other motifs, as in the following example.

The *6-note grouping* is the same as on *page 66*. It consists of four accented single strokes with the hands, followed by two bass-drum beats at the end of the figure. The left hand stays on the rack tom, and the right hand alternates between the snare drum and floor tom.

As you play the figure alternately with a *shuffle groove*, the basic feel will be eighth-note triplets. The *4-note grouping* is still **R L L F**.

"Two Bass-Drum Beats" 1 (Original figure)

6-note grouping

R L R L F F

4-note grouping

R L L F

Now combine the 6- and 4-note groupings with help from **Reading Text 5** (*6- and 4-Note Groupings Using Sixteenth-Note Triplets*). The basis of the following fill is *Combination 1* of this reading text.

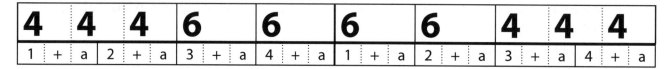

4			4			4			6			6			6			6			4			4			4		
1	+	a	2	+	a	3	+	a	4	+	a	1	+	a	2	+	a	3	+	a	4	+	a			

"Two Bass-Drum Beats" 2 (Combination 1 from Reading Text 5)   CD 35

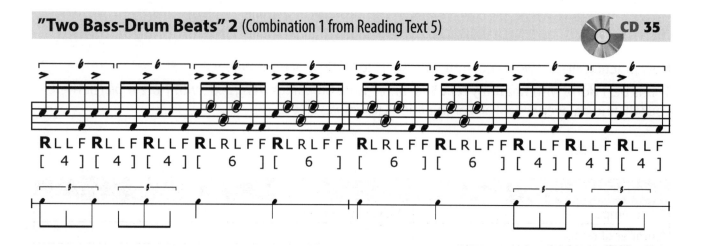

R L L F **R** L L F **R** L L F **R** L R L F F **R** L R L F F **R** L R L F F **R** L R L F F **R** L L F **R** L L F **R** L L F
[4] [4] [4] [6   ] [6   ] [6   ] [6   ] [4] [4] [4]

Practice Steps	
Start tempo	Quarter note = 60
Number of tempos	3
Number of rounds per tempo	Every fill of the reading text 2 times
Musical form	2-bar groove + 2-bar fill
Count out loud	Quarter note and "click" | eighth-note triplets when required
Duration of exercise	Around 15 minutes

In *Chapter 5,* we will go further with fills using *32nd notes*.

Fills Using 32nd Notes

In this chapter, I will show you some different ways to play fills using *32nd notes*.

Fills Using 32nd Notes 1 (8- and 4-Note Groupings)

As with the beginning of *Chapters 2 and 4*, start with a figure that is a quarter note long. In 32nd notes, this equals *eight* beats.

So you don't need to learn a completely new motif, I've used the previously covered *6-note grouping (see the Sixteenth-Note Triplet Fill (Original figure) on page 61)*, preceded by two beats.

The 6-note grouping was the sticking **R L R L L F**. Play two more beats in front of it (**R L**) to get the following original figure:

32nd Notes 1 (Original figure)

The original figure is over one bar. With the exception of the double strokes in the left hand, all beats in this fill are accented, but I've left the accents out for the sake of clarity.

32nd Notes 1.1 (Original figure over one bar)   **CD 36**

RLRLRLLF

The original figure is our *8-note grouping*. Make sure you play the unaccented notes quietly. The bass-drum beat at the end should be about as loud as the accents. Next, displace the 8-note grouping by one eighth note from the downbeat to the eighth-note offbeat. That means the 8-note grouping now begins on beat 1+ (the offbeat). The challenge: Start the fill on beat 1+, and hear how different it sounds in relation to the quarter-note pulse.

Play a snare-drum accent on beat 1 and then the 8-note grouping on beat 1+.

32nd Notes 1.2 (8-note grouping displaced by one eighth note)

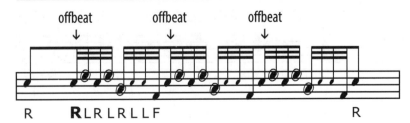

Now let's add *32nd Notes 1.1* and *1.2* together to make a *two-bar fill*.

Although the subdivision of the fills is 32nd notes, the underlying rhythm is based on eighth notes. The rhythm of the fills is clarified in *line 2*.

32nd Notes 1.3 (Combination of 32nd Notes 1.1 and 1.2)

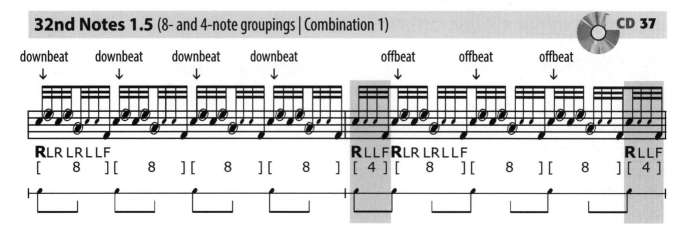

Tip

Eighth notes are the underlying rhythm of the 8- and 4-note groupings using 32nd notes.

Chapter 2 (page 31) describes how you can make the underlying rhythm clearer to yourself.

Next, play a better transition between the two positions of the original figure. Instead of the eighth note on the snare drum (*see 32nd Notes 1.3*, bar 2, beats 1 and 4+), play the following (previously covered) *4-Note Grouping Using 32nd Notes*.

32nd Notes 1.4 (4-note grouping)

I haven't written the accent in the following example (*as the accents in the 8-note grouping*) ... but you should play it.

Now add the *4-note grouping* to the *two-bar fill* you already know from *32nd Notes 1.3*.
Start the fill with the *8-note grouping* on beat 1 (the downbeat). On beat 1 of the second bar, play the 4-note grouping once, directly followed by the 8-note grouping, which you now play on the offbeat (1+). To finish, play the 4-note grouping on beat 4+. All 4-note groupings are marked in **gray**.

32nd Notes 1.5 (8- and 4-note groupings | Combination 1)   CD 37

Now *alternate* the 8- and 4-note groupings. As a result, the position of the 8-note grouping always changes between the downbeat and the offbeat.

32nd Notes 1.6 (8- and 4-note groupings | Combination 2)

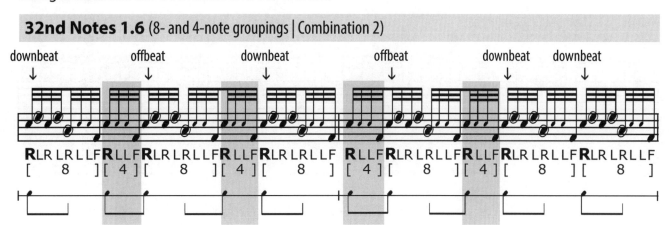

32nd Notes 1.7 shows another possibility as to how to combine the 8- and 4-note groupings. Start with the 4-note grouping, which means that the first 8-note grouping starts on the offbeat.

32nd Notes 1.7 (8- and 4-note groupings | Combination 3)

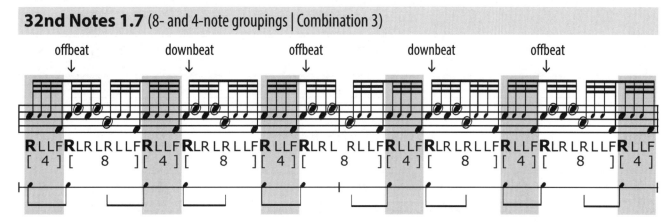

Cross-Reference

There is a snare-drum exercise for 8- and 4-note groupings that aims to further the basic rhythmic idea (*see Appendix, page 138*). It is useful to play the snare-drum exercises and fills during the same practice session.

Try to play the following fills using only the numbers (in *square brackets* below the notation) so you can gradually get rid of the notes. The stickings are already well known, so I've left them out of the following examples. You should only look at the notes if you need a visual.

32nd Notes 1.8 (8- and 4-note groupings | Combination 4)

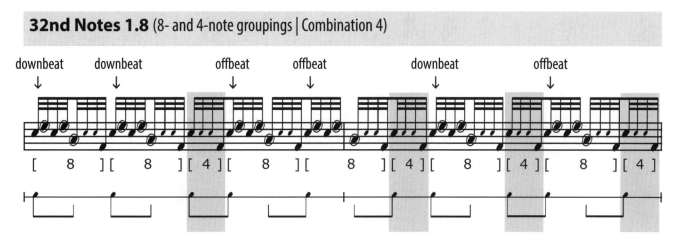

32nd Notes 1.9 (8- and 4-note groupings | Combination 5)

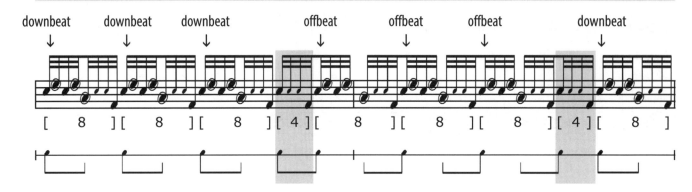

To be rhythmically confident when dealing with 8- and 4-note groupings, practice additional combinations by working with place holders (the numbers 8 and 4). The following four combinations of the 8- and 4-note groupings each represent a *two-bar fill* in $\frac{4}{4}$ time.

32nd Notes 1.10 (8- and 4-note groupings | Combination 6)

8		4	8		8		4	8		8		4	8		4
1	+	2	+	3	+	4	+	1	+	2	+	3	+	4	+

32nd Notes 1.11 (8- and 4-note groupings | Combination 7)

4	8		8		8		4	8		8		4	8		4
1	+	2	+	3	+	4	+	1	+	2	+	3	+	4	+

32nd Notes 1.12 (8- and 4-note groupings | Combination 8)

4	8		4	4	8		4	8		4	8		8		4
1	+	2	+	3	+	4	+	1	+	2	+	3	+	4	+

32nd Notes 1.13 (8- and 4-note groupings | Combination 9)

8		8		4	4	4	8		4	4	8		4	8	
1	+	2	+	3	+	4	+	1	+	2	+	3	+	4	+

The Principle

Play the *8-note grouping* using 32nd notes. In combination with the *4-note grouping*, the *8-note grouping* always alternates between the downbeat and the offbeat.

Subdivision of fills: **32nd notes**

Grid of underlying rhythm: **Eighth notes**

And so it continues:

Now practice all two-bar combinations using the instructions below.

This works best with **Reading Text 6** (*8- and 4-Note Groupings Using 32nd Notes*). There you will find an overview of all combinations (*examples 1.5 – 1.13*).

Practice Steps	
Start tempo	Eighth note = 100
Number of tempos	3
Number of rounds per tempo	Every fill of the reading text 2 times
Musical form	2-bar groove + 2-bar fill
Count out loud	Quarter note and "click" | eighth notes when required
Duration of exercise	Around 15 minutes

Tip

Two-bar fills using 32nd notes are very long, which is good for practicing. If you prefer to play *one-bar fills*, simply end the combinations from **Reading Text 6** (*8- and 4-Note Groupings Using 32nd Notes*) after one bar.

We can also apply this rhythmic concept to different motifs, such as the following example.

At the beginning of the 8-note grouping play a *six-stroke roll* (**R L L R R L**), followed by two bass-drum beats at the end of the figure. Both hands stay on the snare drum. The *4-note grouping* is **R L L F**, where the right hand plays the floor tom.

"Two Bass-Drum Beats" 1 (Original figure)

8-note grouping

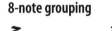

R L L R R L F F

4-note grouping

R L L F

Now combine both groups with the help of **Reading Text 6** (*8- and 4-Note Groupings Using 32nd Notes*). *Combination 2* of this reading text is the basis for the following fill.

8		4	8		4	8		4	8		4	8		8	
1	+	2	+	3	+	4	+	1	+	2	+	3	+	4	+

"Two Bass-Drum Beats" 2 (Combination 2 from Reading Text 6)

CD 39

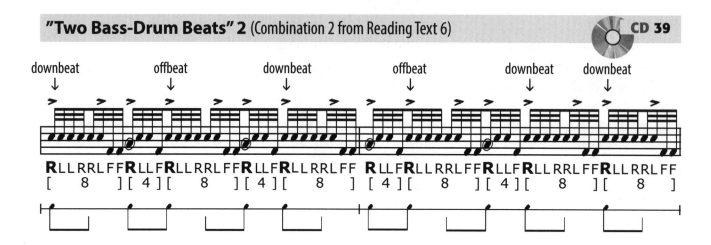

To make an easy transition back to the groove possible after the above fill, replace the last two bass-drum beats with the hands (**R L**). This will allow you to comfortably play the bass drum on beat 1 of your grooves.

Practice Steps	
Start tempo	Eighth note = 100
Number of tempos	3
Number of rounds per tempo	Every fill of the reading text 2 times
Musical form	2-bar groove + 2-bar fill
Count out loud	Quarter note and "click" | eighth notes when required
Duration of exercise	Around 15 minutes

The underlying rhythm of the 32nd-note fills in this chapter is based on straight eighth notes. Next is an idea in which the rhythm is based on sixteenth notes.

Fills Using 32nd Notes 2 (6- and 4-Note Groupings)

Moving forward, the underlying rhythm of fills changes from eighth notes to sixteenth notes.

The subdivision of fills remains unchanged, meaning that the following fills continue to consist of 32nd notes.

You already know the *6- and 4-note groupings* from the *Fills Using Sixteenth-Note Triplets 3* (*see pages 71 to 75*). We will use the same exact motifs here. First, it is useful to be able to play motifs you have already learned in other subdivisions, and second, it sounds extremely good (which is, of course, much more important than being "useful").

Let's take the following, previously covered *6-note grouping* as the original figure:

32nd Notes 2 (Original figure)

Now play the 6-note grouping over *one* bar. You can see the underlying rhythm in *line 2,* which—as already explained—is based on sixteenth notes from here.

32nd Notes 2.1 (Original figure over one bar)   **CD 40**

Now the 4-note grouping comes into play (also previously covered).

32nd Notes 2.2 (4-note grouping)

We now combine the 4-note grouping with the 6-note grouping to make *one-bar fills*. To do that, play the combination 6–6–4 twice. (All 4-note groupings are marked **gray**.)

32nd Notes 2.3 (6- and 4-note groupings | Combination 1)   **CD 41**

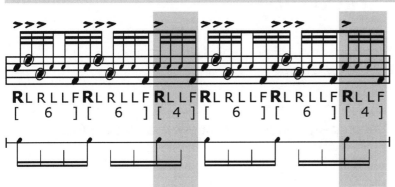

Tip

Sixteenth notes are the underlying rhythm here. The *Preliminary Notes* (*see pages 6 and 7*) describe how you can make the underlying sixteenth-note rhythm clearer to yourself.

In the following fill, play the *combination 4–6–6* twice:

32nd Notes 2.4 (6- and 4-note groupings | Combination 2)

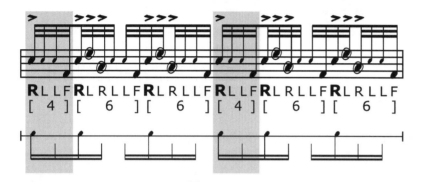

In the next fill, you will always play *alternating* 6- and 4-note groupings.

32nd Notes 2.5 (6- and 4-note groupings | Combination 3)

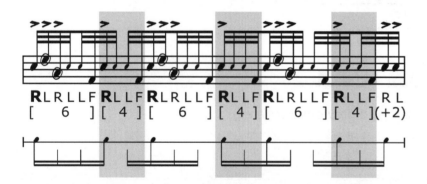

32nd Notes 2.6 (6- and 4-note groupings | Combination 4)

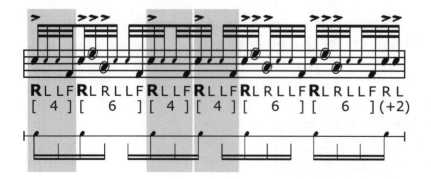

If you can hear the previous fills over one bar properly, you should continue with *two-bar fills*.

The first *two-bar fill* only consists of the *6-note grouping*.

32nd Notes 2.7 (6-note grouping over two bars)

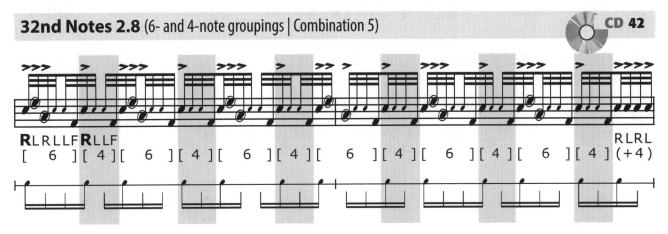

We can't miss the *4-note grouping* from the *two-bar fills*. First, keep *alternating* between 6- and 4-note groupings.

32nd Notes 2.8 (6- and 4-note groupings | Combination 5) CD 42

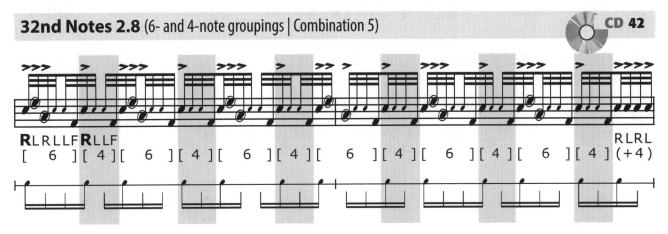

In the following fill, start with the *4-note grouping*, and then keep *alternating* between the 6- and 4-note groupings.

32nd Notes 2.9 (6- and 4-note groupings | Combination 6)

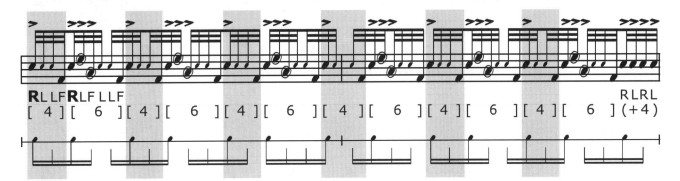

Cross-Reference

On the theme of *6- and 4-note groupings using 32nd notes*, there's a snare-drum exercise in the *Appendix*, with the aim of furthering the basic rhythmic idea (*see page 139*).
It is useful to practice the snare-drum exercise and fills during the same practice session.

Play the next two fills using only the numbers (in *square brackets* below the notation) so you can slowly get rid of the notes.

The stickings are well known by now, so I've left them out of the next two fills. You shouldn't look at the notes anymore, as they're only there in case you need a visual.

6 = **R L R L L F**

4 = **R L L F**

32nd Notes 2.10 (6- and 4-note groupings | Combination 7)

[6][4][6][6][4][4][6][6][4][6][6][4](+2)

32nd Notes 2.11 (6- and 4-note groupings | Combination 8)

[4][6][4][6][6][4][4][6][4][6][6][6](+2)

To be sure you're rhythmically comfortable with the 6- and 4-note groupings, practice further combinations by working with place holders (the numbers 6 and 4). The following four combinations of the 6- and 4-note groupings each represent a *two-bar fill* in $\frac{4}{4}$ time.

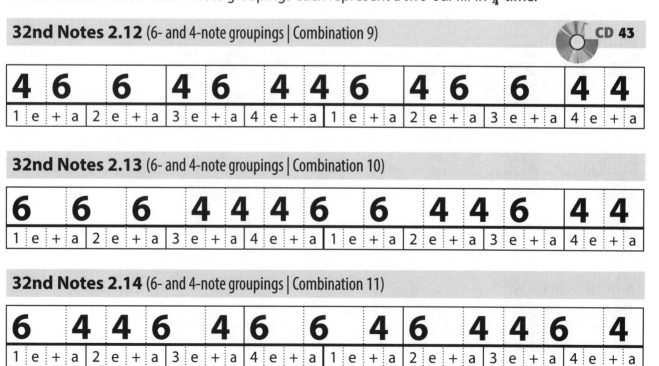

32nd Notes 2.12 (6- and 4-note groupings | Combination 9)   **CD 43**

4	6		6	4	6		4	4	6		4	6		6		4	4
1	e	+	a	2	e	+	a	3	e	+	a	4	e	+	a	1	e	+	a	2	e	+	a	3	e	+	a	4	e	+	a

32nd Notes 2.13 (6- and 4-note groupings | Combination 10)

| 6 | | 6 | | 6 | | 4 | 4 | 6 | | 6 | | 4 | 4 | 6 | | 4 | 4 |
| 1 e + a | 2 e + a | 3 e + a | 4 e + a | 1 e + a | 2 e + a | 3 e + a | 4 e + a |

32nd Notes 2.14 (6- and 4-note groupings | Combination 11)

| 6 | 4 | 4 | 6 | 4 | 6 | 6 | 4 | 6 | 4 | 4 | 6 | 4 |
| 1 e + a | 2 e + a | 3 e + a | 4 e + a | 1 e + a | 2 e + a | 3 e + a | 4 e + a |

In the following example, you'll see "+2" at the end. This means that two beats are missing until the two bars are complete. Simply play **R L** here (two 32nd notes).

32nd Notes 2.15 (6- and 4-note groupings | Combination 12)

6	6	4	4	6	6	4	4	6	6	4	6	+2

1	e	+	a	2	e	+	a	3	e	+	a	4	e	+	a	1	e	+	a	2	e	+	a	3	e	+	a	4	e	+	a

The Principle

Play *6- and 4-note groupings using 32nd notes*. This combination will produce interesting rhythms in the *sixteenth-note grid*.

Subdivision of fills: **32nd notes**

Grid of underlying rhythm: **Sixteenth notes**

And so it continues:

Now practice all two-bar combinations using the instructions below.

This works best with **Reading Text 7** (*6- and 4-Note Groupings Using 32nd Notes*). There you will find an overview of all the combinations (*examples 2.7–2.15*).

Practice Steps	
Start tempo	Eighth note = 100
Number of tempos	3
Number of rounds per tempo	Every fill of the reading text 2 times
Musical form	2-bar groove + 2-bar fill
Count out loud	Quarter note and "click"	sixteenth notes when required
Duration of exercise	Around 15 minutes

Transfer this rhythmic concept to other motifs, as in the following example.

For example:

The *6-note grouping* consists of four single strokes with the hands, followed by two bass-drum beats at the end of the figure. The *left hand* stays on the rack tom, while the *right hand* alternates between the snare drum and the floor tom.

The *4-note grouping* consists of two accents on the snare drum, followed by two bass-drum beats.

"Two Bass-Drum Beats" 1 (Original figure)

6-note grouping

R L R L F F

4-note grouping

R L F F

Now combine both groups with **Reading Text 7** (*6- and 4-Note Groupings Using 32nd Notes*).
Here is *Combination 2* of this reading text as the basis for the following fill.
The 4-note groupings are marked in **gray**.

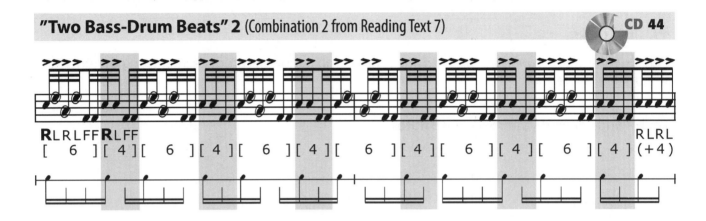

"**Two Bass-Drum Beats**" **2** (Combination 2 from Reading Text 7)   **CD 44**

Practice Steps	
Start tempo	Eighth note = 100
Number of tempos	3
Number of rounds per tempo	Every fill of the reading text 2 times
Musical form	2-bar groove + 2-bar fill
Count out loud	Quarter note and "click" | sixteenth notes when required
Duration of exercise	Around 15 minutes

Fills in 3-, 5-, and 7-Note Groupings

This chapter is about *3-, 5-, and 7-note groupings*.

First, let's dedicate ourselves to the *3-note groupings* you already know from *Chapter 1*.
There you played **R L F** using sixteenth notes, and orchestrated it in different ways.

Now, play another motif using sixteenth notes:

The right hand plays the ride cymbal together with the bass drum, followed by two ghost notes on the snare drum.

Fills in 3-, 5-, and 7-Note Groupings (3-note grouping | original figure)

Play the following figure over *two* bars. You can see the underlying rhythm in *line 2*.

Fills in 3-, 5-, and 7-Note Groupings 1 (3-note grouping over two bars) CD 45

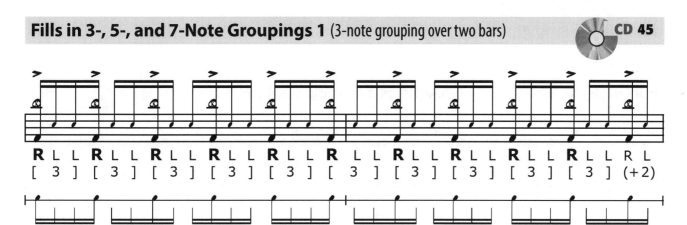

The following *5-note grouping* shows the most common way of accenting a group of 5. Play accents on the *first* and *third* beats of the 5-note grouping. These accents are obviously not the only way in which to play a 5-note grouping, but it is—as already said—the best-known way.

Fills in 3-, 5-, and 7-Note Groupings 2 (5-note grouping | original figure)

Now play the 5-note grouping over two bars. The underlying rhythm in *line 2* always shows the beginning of the 5-note grouping.

Fills in 3-, 5-, and 7-Note Groupings 3 (5-note grouping over two bars) CD 46

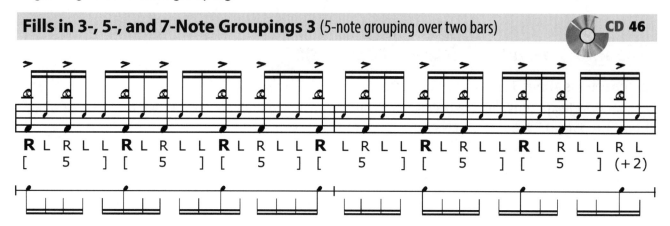

The *7-note grouping* is similar to the 5-note grouping. The accents are on the *first, third,* and *fifth* beats of the 7-note grouping, but, again, this isn't the only way you can play a 7-note grouping.

Fills in 3-, 5-, and 7-Note Groupings 4 (7-note grouping | original figure)

Fills in 3-, 5-, and 7-Note Groupings 5 (7-note grouping over two bars) CD 47

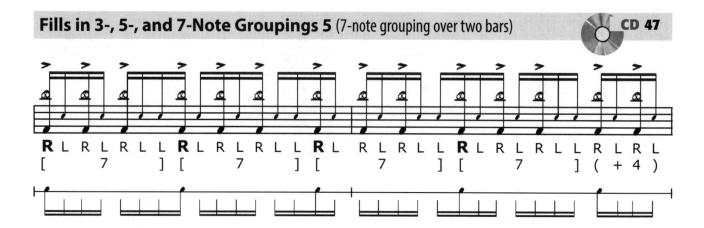

The goal is to now combine all three building blocks (*3-, 5-, and 7-note groupings*). When you dedicate yourself to this,

- you obtain a tool that allows you to think of very creative fills (and grooves).
- your basic understanding and feeling of rhythm will be greatly improved.
- you improve your ability to improvise.

For an easy way to start combining, first start with two of the three groups. I suggest the *3- and 5-note groupings*.

Combinations of 3- and 5-Note Groupings

Fills in 3-, 5-, and 7-Note Groupings 6 (3- and 5-note groupings | Combination 1)   CD 48

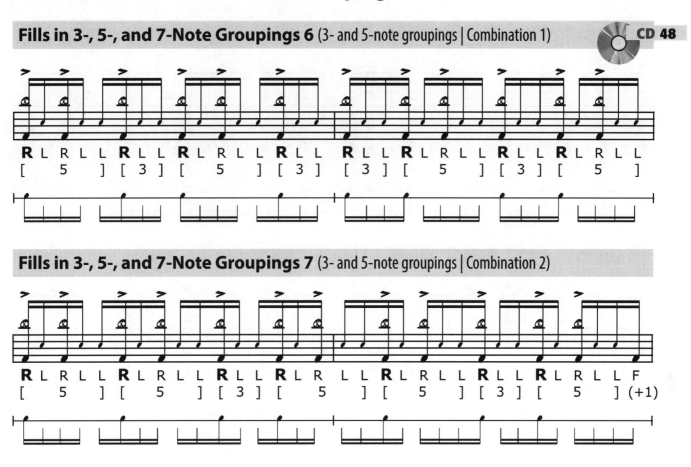

Fills in 3-, 5-, and 7-Note Groupings 7 (3- and 5-note groupings | Combination 2)

Combinations of 3- and 7-Note Groupings

Fills in 3-, 5-, and 7-Note Groupings 8 (3- and 7-note groupings | Combination 1)   CD 49

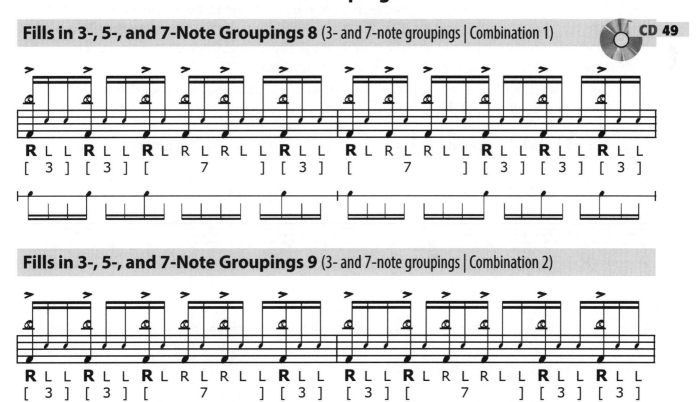

Fills in 3-, 5-, and 7-Note Groupings 9 (3- and 7-note groupings | Combination 2)

Combinations of 5- and 7-Note Groupings

Fills in 3-, 5-, and 7-Note Groupings 10 (5- and 7-note groupings | Combination 1) **CD 50**

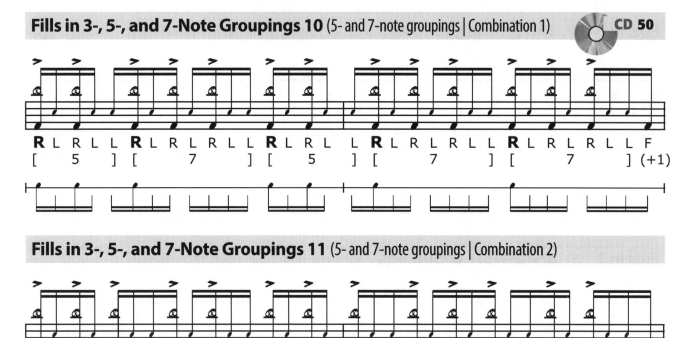

Fills in 3-, 5-, and 7-Note Groupings 11 (5- and 7-note groupings | Combination 2)

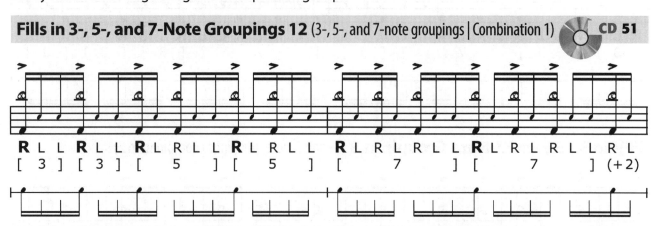

Reading Text 8 (*3-, 5-, and 7-Note Groupings Using Sixteenth Notes I*) has an overview of the preliminary exercises (*Fills in 3-, 5-, and 7-Note Groupings 6 to 11*), and three further combinations in this style you should use to practice. It's not a matter of playing the fills from **Reading Text 8** at an especially high tempo, it's more about being rhythmically secure! Once you've attained that, continue with the following combinations of all three groups.

Here are combinations of all three groups in two-bar examples. In *line 2*, the underlying rhythm always shows the beginning of the respective group.

Fills in 3-, 5-, and 7-Note Groupings 12 (3-, 5-, and 7-note groupings | Combination 1) **CD 51**

Tip

Remind yourself of the underlying rhythm from time to time, as described at the beginning of this book on *pages 6 and 7*.

Fills in 3-, 5-, and 7-Note Groupings 13 (3-, 5-, and 7-note groupings | Combination 2)

Counting Out Loud

The *most effective* way to make the rhythms of these groups (and others) your own is to *count out loud*! Without a permanent overview of the rhythms in relation to the quarter-note pulse, the exercises are mechanical and unmusical. It might be laborious to start off with, but you will learn another basic skill that can be used in many different contexts. Unfortunately, playing the left foot on the quarter-note pulse with the hi-hat doesn't replace counting out loud.

Using *Fills in 3-, 5-, and 7-Note Groupings 13* from above as an example, here is my approach:

1. Count all sixteenth notes out loud. This lead-in should make it easier. As soon as that feels comfortable, move ahead with step 2.

2. Now leave out the sixteenth-note subdivisions, and only count the quarter notes out loud. As soon as that goes well, go ahead with step 3.

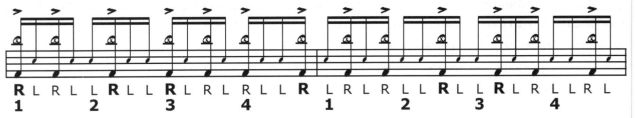

3. Now change the counting of the quarter note to a percussive sound. Say "click" for every quarter note.

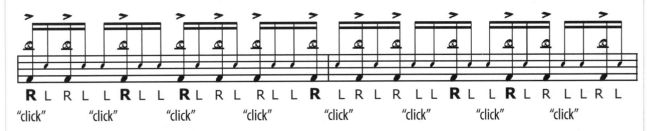

There are two reasons for saying "click."
- You have to be more precise, as the sound is more percussive than saying the numbers out loud.
- Because you don't pronounce the quarter notes out loud anymore, you have to internalize where beat 1 is. Once you have internalized this, you will always hear or feel exactly where you are in the bar.

To be certain you're comfortable playing with *3-, 5-, and 7-Note Groupings*, practice other combinations using this principle by working with place holders (the numbers 3, 5, and 7).

Reading Text 9 (*3-, 5-, and 7-Note Groupings Using Sixteenth Notes II*) shows nine combinations of 3-, 5-, and 7-note groupings you should now practice.

Practice Steps	
Start tempo	Quarter note = 82
Number of tempos	4
Number of rounds per tempo	Every fill of the reading text 2 times
Musical form	2-bar groove + 2-bar fill
Count out loud	Quarter note and "click" | sixteenth notes when required
Duration of exercise	Around 15 minutes

The Principle

Play *3-, 5-, and 7-note groupings using sixteenth notes.*

Because all three groups are odd, they always alternate between the *eighth-note downbeats* and the *sixteenth-note offbeats.*

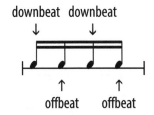

Subdivision of fills: **Sixteenth notes**
Grid of underlying rhythm: **Sixteenth notes**

3-, 5-, and 7-note groupings are a rhythmic concept you should absolutely use in other ways. Here is an application with a *new orchestration*, but with the same stickings.

The 3-note grouping doesn't change.

In the *5-note grouping,* accent the *first two beats* on the snare drum (or toms).

In the *7-note grouping,* accent the *first four beats* on the snare drum (or toms).

Fills in 3-, 5-, and 7-Note Groupings—Orchestration 2

Orchestration 2 (3-, 5-, and 7-note groupings \| original figure)

3-note grouping

R L L

5-note grouping

R L R L L

7-note grouping

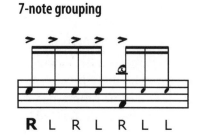

R L R L R L L

Now combine these three groups with the help of **Reading Text 9** (*3-, 5-, and 7-Note Groupings Using Sixteenth Notes II*). *Combination 1* of this text is the basis for the following fill.

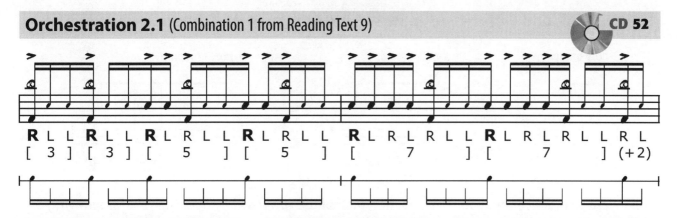

Orchestration 2.1 (Combination 1 from Reading Text 9)   CD 52

Practice Steps	
Start tempo	Quarter note = 82
Number of tempos	4
Number of rounds per tempo	Every fill of the reading text 2 times
Musical form	2-bar groove + 2-bar fill
Count out loud	Quarter note and "click" | sixteenth notes when required
Duration of exercise	Around 15 minutes

Nerd Section

3-note groupings resolve after *three bars.*

5-note groupings resolve after *five bars.*

7-note groupings resolve after *seven bars.*

This is *independent* from the time signature! So in a bar of $\frac{5}{4}$, the 3-note grouping would also repeat itself after three bars.

Exception: All time signatures in which the count of the time signature is the same as the grouping. In these instances, the groupings repeat themselves after one bar.

If you play a 3-note grouping in a bar of $\frac{3}{4}$, it repeats itself after one bar. The same goes for a 5-note grouping in a bar of $\frac{5}{8}$.

Each rhythmic concept can be applied in infinite ways. This can be seen positively:
"It's unbelievable that such an inexhaustible reservoir of ideas and possibilities are offered here."
Or negatively: *"There are too many possibilities, and I don't even know where to begin."*

The more conceptual approaches you follow on the instrument, the more obvious it will become that the possibilities are infinite. The only thing that will help is for you to decide which things you like the most, and that will bring the most fun. As long as these things fascinate you and you do well, you don't need to think about other possibilities. Then, when you have some free capacity again, have a look at some other options. Be guided by fun and your passion, and be diligent and disciplined!

Fills in 3-, 5-, and 7-Note Groupings Using Eighth-Note Triplets

A note for those especially interested:

The concept of the *3-, 5-, and 7-note groupings* can be transferred to *all subdivisions*. Eighth-note triplets are the next logical subdivision.

The stickings and orchestration of the groups remain unchanged—it's "only" the subdivision that changes.

Fills in 3-, 5-, and 7-Note Groupings Using Eighth-Note Triplets (Original figure)

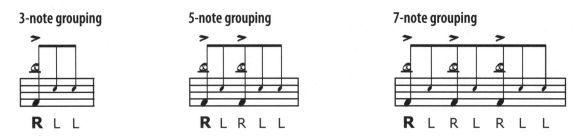

If you want to practice this, you must practice each of the groups *individually* first before moving on to the combinations. A two-bar combination might look like this:

Fills in 3-, 5-, and 7-Note Groupings Using Eighth-Note Triplets 1

3	5		7			3	5		+1
1 + a	2 + a	3 + a	4 + a	1 + a	2 + a	3 + a	4 + a		

Here is what the combination looks like when written out:

 CD 53

Fills in 3-, 5-, and 7-Note Groupings Using Eighth-Note Triplets 1.2 (Combination Fill)

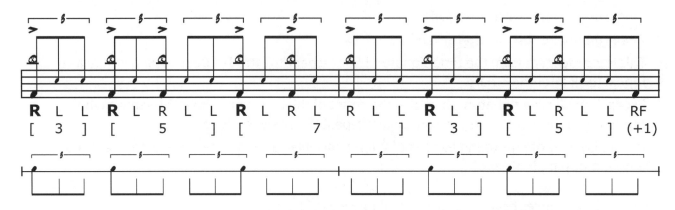

Reading Texts 10 and **11** are intended for practicing 3-, 5-, and 7-note groupings using eighth-note triplets:

In **Reading Text 10** (*3-, 5-, and 7-Note Groupings Using Eighth-Note Triplets I*), you will find combinations of two of the three groupings.

Reading Text 11 (*3-, 5-, and 7-Note Groupings Using Eighth-Note Triplets II*) shows combinations of all three groupings using eighth-note triplets.

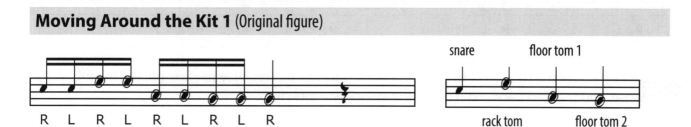

Moving Around the Kit

In this chapter, I'll show you some fills you can use to move around the kit easily.

Moving Around the Kit 1: Clockwise and Counterclockwise

As a right-handed player, you would play most fills in a *clockwise* direction.

Example: Your fill starts on the snare drum, the rack tom and floor tom follow, and it ends on a crash cymbal. In other words, it moves in a *clockwise* direction.

Fills in a *counterclockwise* direction are quite rare, and so that's why I'll go into more detail here.

Here is a fill in a *clockwise* direction, which serves as the basis for the following fills.

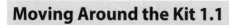

Moving Around the Kit 1 (Original figure)

Now play the same figure in a *counterclockwise* direction without changing the sticking. To play the fill quickly, play an odd number of beats on the deepest tom.

Option 1: Play one beat on the deepest tom, and then lead with the left hand (*the left hand is first on each tom*).

Moving Around the Kit 1.1

The odd number of tom beats at the beginning of the fill will prevent your hands from getting mixed up with each other.

Alternate playing this fill with the original figure in a *two-bar fill*.

Moving Around the Kit 1.2   CD 54

Option 2: Play three beats on your deepest tom, and then lead with the *left hand*.

Moving Around the Kit 1.3

R L R L R L R L R

Alternate this fill with the *original figure (Around the Kit 1)* in a *two-bar fill*.

Moving Around the Kit 1.4

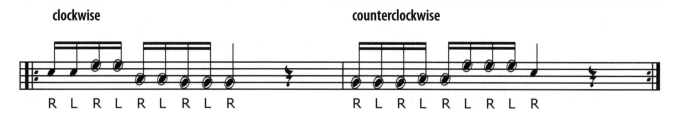

Now let's transfer the basic idea to fills using *sixteenth-note triplets*. Play the first part of the fill *clockwise*, and then go back again in a *counterclockwise* direction.

Moving Around the Kit 1.5

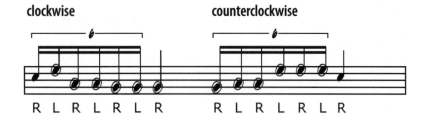

Next, change the rhythm of the fills. Instead of playing quarter notes on beats 2 and 4, play *eighth notes* at the end of the phrase. Play *clockwise on the downbeat* and *counterclockwise on the offbeat*. The stickings stay the same. Continue to play singles.

Moving Around the Kit 1.6

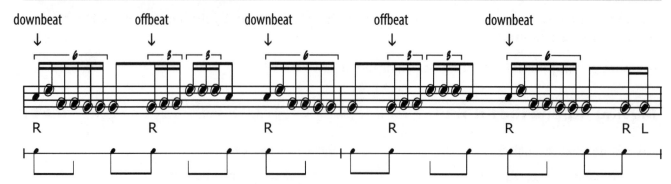

Now, let's add the bass drum. Fill each gap with two bass-drum beats. Everything else stays the same.

Moving Around the Kit 1.7

www.jostnickel.com

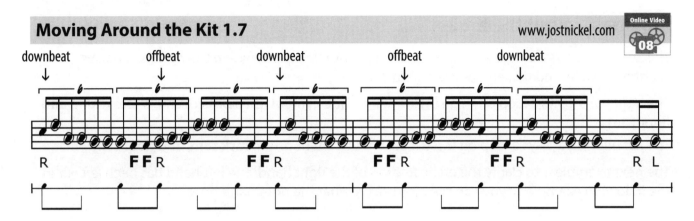

Now let's play a longer figure, which is *clockwise for the first half* and *counterclockwise for the second*. The sticking and orchestration are unchanged. Here are two preliminary exercises.

Moving Around the Kit 1.8 (Preliminary Exercise 1)

In *Preliminary Exercise 2*, play the exact same figure, now *displaced by one eighth note*. The fill now begins on beat 1+ (offbeat).

Moving Around the Kit 1.9 (Preliminary Exercise 2)

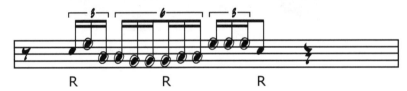

Now let's combine both preliminary exercises into a *two-bar fill*. Therefore, the figure alternates between the downbeat and the offbeat.

Moving Around the Kit 1.10

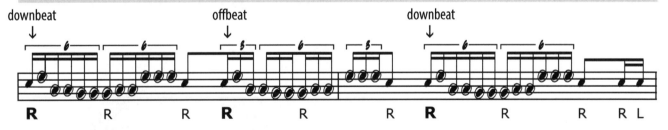

The bass drum gets added last here as well. Fill the gaps with *two bass-drum beats* each. Everything else stays the same.

Moving Around the Kit 1.11

www.jostnickel.com

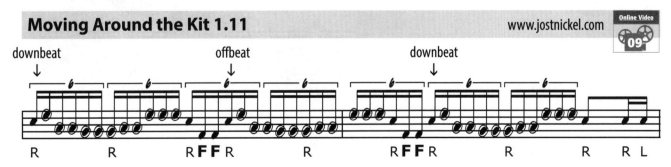

Moving Around the Kit 2

This section covers a *6-note grouping using sixteenth-note triplets,* where the right hand plays *counterclockwise* and the left hand plays *clockwise.*

The *right hand* plays a loop on three instruments: **Ride cymbal (plus bass drum), snare drum, and floor tom**

The *left hand* also plays a loop on three instruments: **Snare drum, rack tom, and floor tom**

The next example is to clarify the orchestration of the right hand. The left hand has been *left out* in the following example so you can see more easily what the right hand does.

Moving Around the Kit 2.1 (Right hand plays the ride cymbal, bass drum, snare drum, and floor tom.)

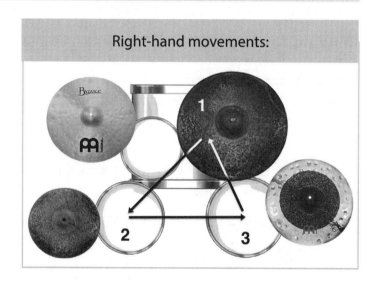

And now the same approach for the left hand. The right hand has been *left out* of the following example so you can see more easily what the left hand does.

Moving Around the Kit 2.2 (Left hand plays the snare drum, rack tom, and floor tom.)

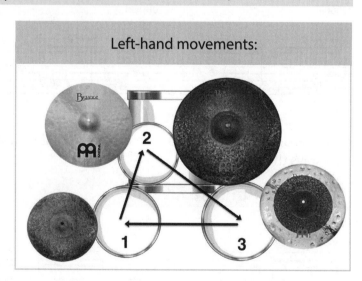

When you play both hands at the same time, it looks like this:

Moving Around the Kit 2.3 (Original figure | both hands together)

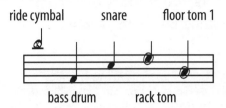

R L R L R L

Play this figure over *one* bar.

Moving Around the Kit 2.4 (Original figure over one bar)

R L R L R L **R** L R L R L **R** L R L R L **R** L R L R L

Now I'd like to show you how to transfer this fill to the concept of the *6- and 3-note groupings in Chapter 4* (*see pages 61 to 65*), where the 6-note grouping changes between the downbeat and the offbeat. You know the 6-note grouping already, so the only thing missing is a 3-note grouping that fits well.

Moving Around the Kit 2.5 (3-note grouping)

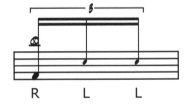

R L L

> Beats 2 and 3 of the 3-note grouping should be played as ghost notes.

Now combine the 6- and 3-note groupings with **Reading Text 4** (*6- and 3-Note Groupings Using Sixteenth-Note Triplets*). *Combination 1* of this reading text is the basis for the following fill.

6		6		6		6		3	6		6		6		3
1	+	2	+	3	+	4	+	1	+	2	+	3	+	4	+

The 3-note groupings are marked in gray. The underlying rhythm is in *line 2*.

Moving Around the Kit 2.6 (Combination 1 from Reading Text 4)   www.jostnickel.com

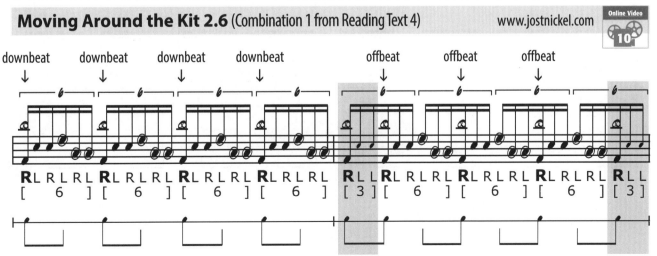

And so it continues:

Now practice all the two-bar combinations using the instructions below.

This works best with **Reading Text 4** (*6- and 3-Note Groupings Using Sixteenth-Note Triplets*).

Practice Steps	
Start tempo	Quarter note = 60
Number of tempos	3
Number of rounds per tempo	Every fill of the reading text 2 times
Musical form	2-bar groove + 2-bar fill
Count out loud	Quarter note and "click" | eighth notes when required
Duration of exercise	Around 15 minutes

Moving Around the Kit 3

Now change the subdivision, and play the 6-note grouping using sixteenth notes, first as a *one-bar fill*.

Moving Around the Kit 3.1

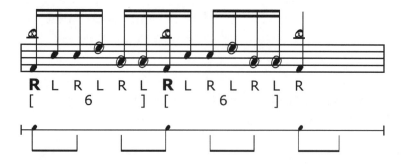

Now try it over *two bars*:

Moving Around the Kit 3.2

www.jostnickel.com

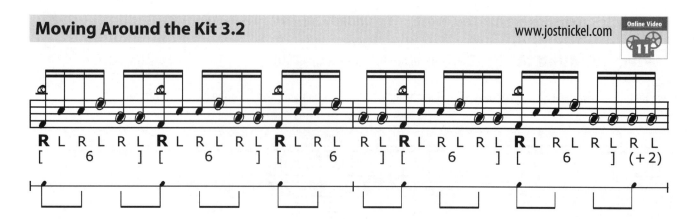

Step–Hit–Hi-Hat

This chapter focuses on a sonic feature I often like to use in fills because you can create delicate sounds with it: it's called the **Step–Hit–Hi-Hat**. The special sound comes from the fact that you first play the hi-hat with your foot (step), followed immediately afterwards with the hand (hit). In *Chapter 2*, there was a little example of the Step–Hit–Hi-Hat with the *Foot Swap* orchestration concept on *page 36*.

Now I'll show you some nice fills based on rhythmic concepts you'll already know from this book. I'll start off with a 9-note grouping using sixteenth-note triplets (*see pages 67 to 70*).

Step–Hit–Hi-Hat 1 (Original figure)

Now repeat the original figure until it creates a *two-bar fill*. Because the original figure is nine sixteenth-note triplets long, it automatically changes between the downbeat and the offbeat. You can see the underlying rhythm of the fill (eighth notes) in *line 2*. At the end of the fill I have changed the sticking so you can play the next beat 1 with the right hand. Every second round is marked in **gray**.

Step–Hit–Hi-Hat 1.1 (Two-bar fill)   CD 56

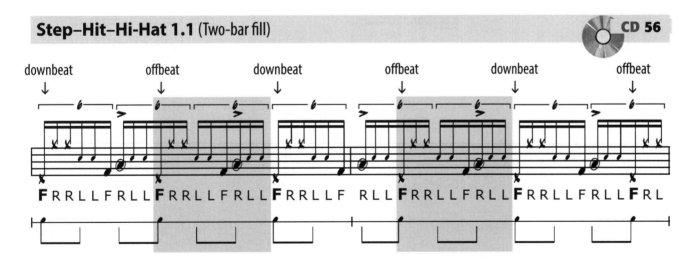

It also sounds good if the fill doesn't start on beat 1. In the next example, the 9-note grouping starts on beat 1+. Again, every second round is marked in **gray**.

Step–Hit–Hi-Hat 1.2 (Original figure begins on beat 1+)

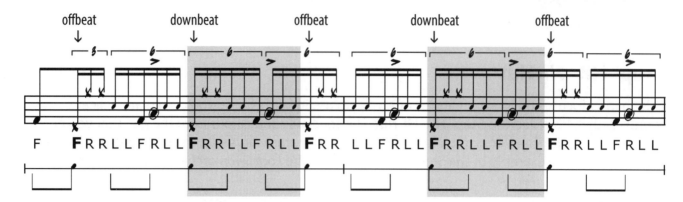

Step–Hit–Hi-Hat 2

Now we come to a Step–Hit fill based on *3-, 5-, and 7-note groupings using sixteenth notes*. The new stickings are a modification of those that were shown at the beginning of *Chapter 6*. Here is a recap of the stickings:

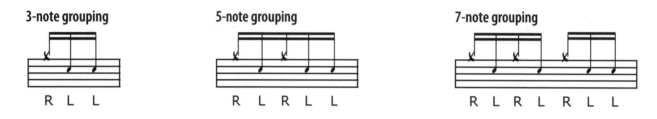

Now double the first note (*every sixteenth note becomes two 32nd notes*). The resulting double beat is split between the left foot (*step*) and the right hand (*hit*). As a result:

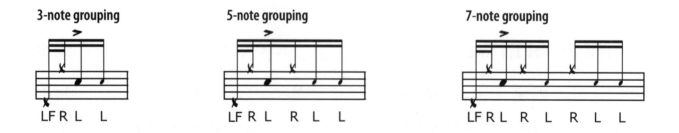

Although the 3-note groupings consist of four notes, nothing changes in duration. They are still three sixteenth notes long and therefore still called a 3-note grouping. The same applies to the 5- and 7-note groupings shown above.

Step–Hit–Hi-Hat 2 (Original figure)

Combine these three groups with **Reading Text 9** (*3-, 5-, and 7-Note Groupings Using Sixteenth Notes II*). *Combination 1* of this reading text is the basis for the following fill.

3	3	5		5		7		7		+2
1 e + a	2 e + a	3 e + a	4 e + a	1 e + a	2 e + a	3 e + a	4 e + a			

You can see the underlying rhythm in *line 2*.

Step–Hit–Hi-Hat 2.1 (Combination 1 from Reading Text 9)

CD 57

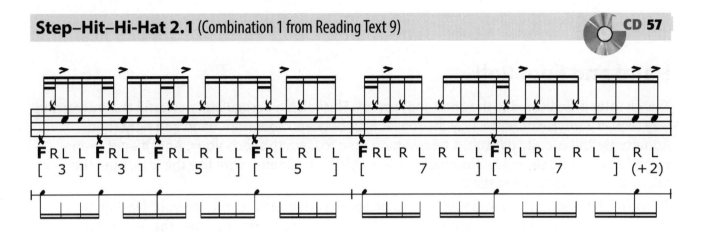

If you like this sound, you should practice all combinations from **Reading Text 9**.

Practice Steps	
Start tempo	Quarter note = 60
Number of tempos	3
Number of rounds per tempo	Every fill of the reading text 2 times
Musical form	2-bar groove + 2-bar fill
Count out loud	Quarter note and "click" | sixteenth notes when required
Duration of exercise	Around 15 minutes

If you find **Reading Text 9** difficult, practice **Reading Text 8** first (*3-, 5-, and 7-Note Groupings Using Sixteenth Notes I*). This is less rhythmically demanding because only two of the three groups are combined.

If you like playing 3-, 5-, and 7-note groupings using eighth-note triplets, take **Reading Text 10** (*3-, 5-, and 7-Note Groupings Using Eighth-Note Triplets I*), in which only two of the three groups are combined, and subsequently **Reading Text 11** (*3-, 5-, and 7-Note Groupings Using Eighth-Note Triplets II*).

Hand and Foot Roll

This chapter is dedicated to the *hand and foot roll*. This roll is a particularly powerful and interesting way to play a *single-stroke roll*. Play the roll (at first) between your right hand and right foot. Admittedly, this is quite difficult. It takes a long time to learn this technique. And, it's not even something I would say every drummer *must* be able to do. Some might like the idea, but others might say, "Oh, I don't need that."

As you're still reading, I assume you'd like to be able to integrate the roll into your playing. Let's start with a preliminary exercise using *triplets*. The right hand starts and plays the floor tom.

In *Preliminary Exercises 1* and *2,* only play the right hand in the first bar. Add the bass drum in bar 2, while keeping the figure in the hand (*including the accents*) unchanged. The hand leads!

I *don't* play the following five preliminary exercises with grooves, as they are purely technical exercises.

Hand and Foot Roll 1 (Preliminary Exercise 1)

Hand and Foot Roll 2 (Preliminary Exercise 2)

In *Preliminary Exercise 3,* combine the second bars of the previous exercises.

Hand and Foot Roll 3 (Preliminary Exercise 3)

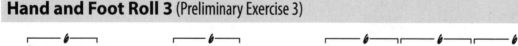

As soon as you feel comfortable with *Preliminary Exercise 3*, you should add in the *left hand* (*rack tom*). This happens in *lines 2* and *3* of the following exercise.

In *line 2,* play the rolls with the *left hand* (*rack tom*) instead of the right.

In *line 3,* play the rolls with *both hands* alternated with an accent on every beat.

Hand and Foot Roll 4 (Preliminary Exercise 4)

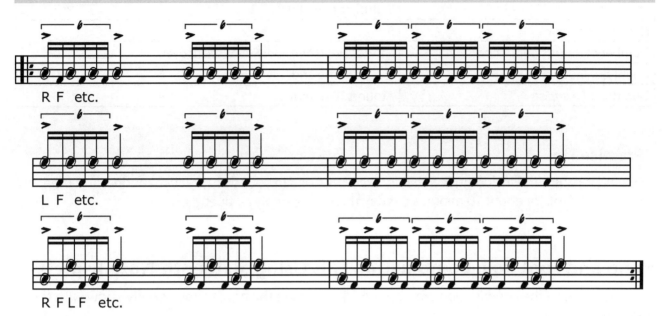

R F etc.

L F etc.

R F L F etc.

Practice Steps	
Start tempo	Quarter note = 60
Number of tempos	5
Number of rounds per tempo	4 times *Hand and Foot Roll 4* (*see above*)
Count out loud	Quarter note and "click"
Duration of exercise	Around 10 minutes

As an alternative to *Preliminary Exercise 4*, you can play the same exercise using 32nd notes (*see Preliminary Exercise 5*). Because both exercises utilize the same technical skill, I would only practice one of the two exercises per day. If you can play both exercises relatively smoothly, you can alternate them daily. If not, focus on one of the two.

Hand and Foot Roll 5 (Preliminary Exercise 5)

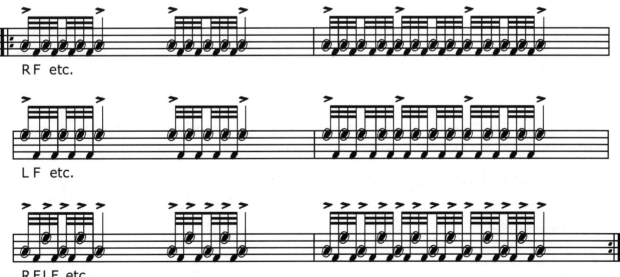

R F etc.

L F etc.

R F L F etc.

Practice Steps	
Start tempo	Eighth note = 100
Number of tempos	5
Number of rounds per tempo	4 times *Hand and Foot Roll 5 (see above)*
Count out loud	Quarter note and "click"
Duration of exercise	Around 10 minutes

Practice Tip

I would recommend including *Preliminary Exercises 4* or *5* in your daily practice routine, and then practice the roll for about 10 minutes per day until you can play it fluently.

Hand and Foot Roll: Combination Fills Using Sixteenth-Note Triplets

Now we come to the *combination exercises*, which combine the figures you already know with the hand and foot roll.

Let's start with a fill using sixteenth-note triplets. Start with *Sixteenth-Note Triplet Fill 1* from *Chapter 4 (see page 61)*, and combine the figure with the hand and foot roll. Play this fill in an alternating manner with *three* or *seven bars* of groove.

Hand and Foot Roll 6 (Combination Exercise 1)

R L R L L F R F etc.

In *Combination Exercise 2*, repeat the first three quarters of the above fills until two bars are complete. The second round is marked in **gray**.

Play this fill in an alternating manner with *two* or *six bars* of groove.

Hand and Foot Roll 7 (Combination Exercise 2)

www.jostnickel.com

R L R L L F R F etc.   **R** L R L L F R F etc.   **R** L R L L F

Now I'd like to show you how to transfer the hand and foot roll to the concept of the *6- and 3-note groupings*, explained in *Chapter 4*, where the 6-note grouping changes between the downbeat and the offbeat. The hand and foot roll is the 6-note grouping.

Hand and Foot Roll 8 (6-note grouping)

R   F   etc.

Combine the *6-note grouping* with a *3-note grouping* by using the previously covered 3-note grouping **R L F**, where both hands are accented.

Hand and Foot Roll 9 (3-note grouping)

R   L   F

Now combine the 6- and 3-note groupings with **Reading Text 4** (*6- and 3-Note Groupings Using Sixteenth-Note Triplets*). *Combination 3* of this reading text is the basis for the following fill.

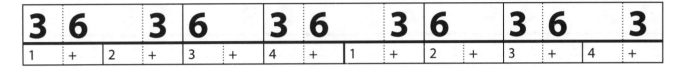

The fill based on this combination can be seen in *Hand and Foot Roll 10*. The 3-note groupings are marked in **gray**, and the underlying rhythm is in *line 2*.

Hand and Foot Roll 10 (Combination Exercise 3 | 6- and 3-note grouping combinations) www.jostnickel.com

It would be advantageous to practice all combinations from **Reading Text 4** (*6- and 3-Note Groupings Using Sixteenth-Note Triplets*).

Hand and Foot Roll: Combination Fills Using 32nd Notes

Obviously, the hand and foot roll can be transferred to the different 32nd-note concepts from *Chapter 5* (*see page 79*). The hand and foot roll is the 8-note grouping:

Hand and Foot Roll 11 (8-note grouping)

R   F   etc.

Combine this 8-note grouping with a 4-note grouping by using the previously covered 4-note grouping **R L L F.**

Hand and Foot Roll 12 (4-note grouping)

Now combine the 8- and 4-note grouping with **Reading Text 6** (*8- and 4-Note Groupings Using 32nd Notes*). *Combination 3* of this reading text is the basis for the following fill.

4	8	4	8	4	8	4	8	4	8	4
1	+	2	+	3	+	4	+	1	+	2	+	3	+	4	+

You can see the fill based on this combination in *Hand and Foot Roll 13*.
The 4-note groupings are marked in **gray**, and the underlying rhythm is in *line 2*.

Hand and Foot Roll 13 (Combination Exercise 4 | 8- and 4-note groupings combination) www.jostnickel.com

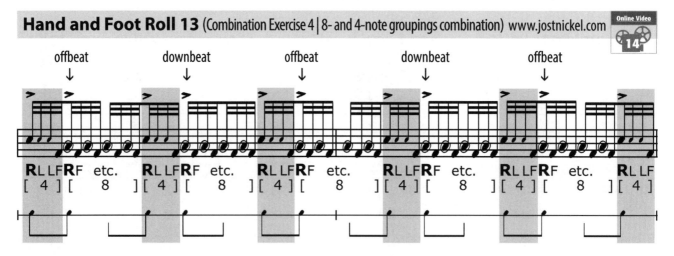

For more fills in this style, practice the rest of the combinations from **Reading Text 6** (*8- and 4-Note Groupings Using Sixteenth Notes*).

Tip

You can also transfer the hand and foot roll to the rhythmic concept of the *6- and 4-note groupings* you already know from *Chapter 5* (*see page 85*).

However, you can't practice everything, nor can you know everything. At the moment, I would say you already understand the idea more than adequately enough. If still interested, you can continue with the hand and foot roll later, but for now, continue with the next chapter.

Cymbal Choke Fills

If you stop a cymbal with your hand immediately after a stroke, it creates the characteristic sound I like to use when playing fills and grooves. It's called a "cymbal choke," and this chapter is dedicated to it.

In the following fills, play *and* choke the cymbal with your left hand. Therefore, you'll need a cymbal you can easily reach with your left hand.

The choke happens at the same time you play the bass drum and is marked with an *arrow* in the notation.

The figure is half a bar long and then starts again from the beginning. I play the cymbal as a prelude to these fills. For me, the first three notes at the beginning are the most characteristic part of the fill.

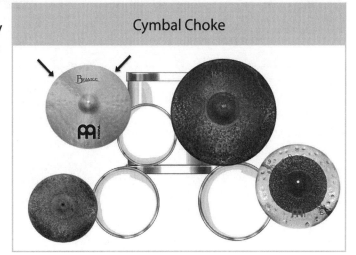

Cymbal Choke

1. **Crash cymbal (without bass drum)**
2. **Snare accent**
3. **Cymbal choke (at the same time as the bass drum)**

Choke 1

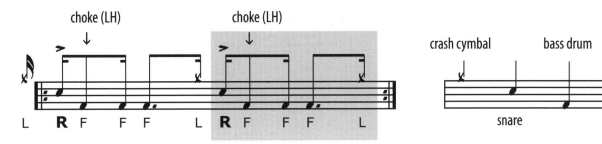

Now the figure is shortened, so it starts again from the beginning, directly after the double beat in the bass drum:

Choke 2 (6-note grouping)

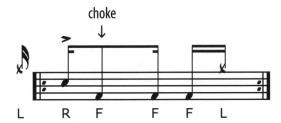

This figure is six sixteenth notes long, so we'll call it a *6-note grouping* and play it over one bar. You can see the underlying rhythm in *line 2*. The second round of the 6-note grouping is marked in **gray**.

Choke 3 (6-note grouping over one bar)

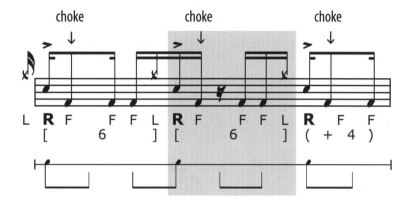

Now play the same figure over *two* bars. Every second round is marked in **gray**.

Choke 4 (6-note grouping over two bars)

www.jostnickel.com

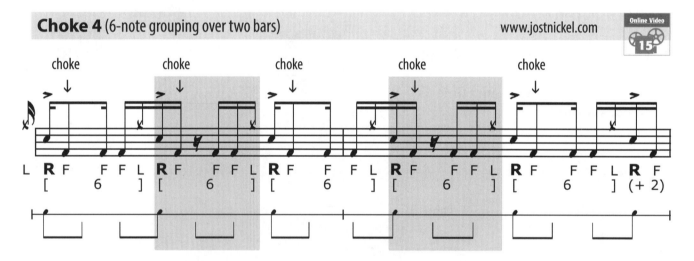

As said before, the first three notes at the beginning make up the fill.

1. **Crash cymbal (without bass drum)**
2. **Snare accent**
3. **Cymbal choke (at the same time as the bass drum)**

Whenever I'm inspired by a motif like this, I try to put it into other rhythmic contexts.

The next example shows the fill in another form as a *5-note grouping*, where the first three beats are unchanged (since they are the sound of the fill).

Choke 5 (5-note grouping)

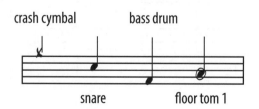

Play the 5-note grouping as a *one-bar fill*. I've included a *flam* at the end of the fill to give it a nice ending.

Choke 6 (5-note grouping over one bar)

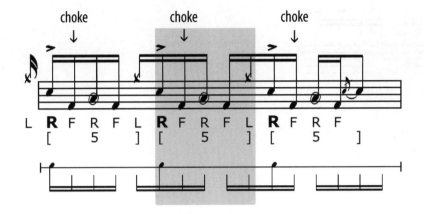

Now play the same figure over *two* bars (every second round is marked in **gray**).

Choke 7 (5-note grouping over two bars)   www.jostnickel.com

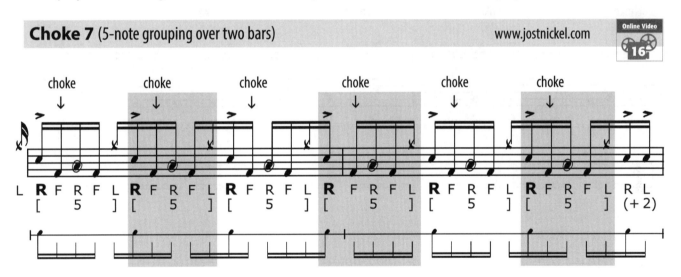

The next example shows the fill in another form as a *7-note grouping*.
The first five beats are identical to the 5-note grouping.

Choke 8 (7-note grouping)

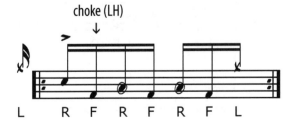

Play the 7-note grouping as a *one-bar fill*.

Choke 9 (7-note grouping over one bar)

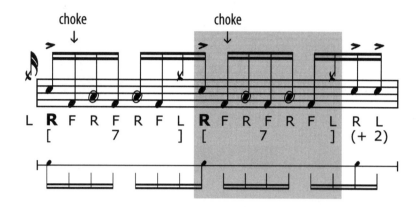

Now play the 7-note grouping over *two bars* (every second round is marked in **gray**).

Choke 10 (7-note grouping over two bars)   www.jostnickel.com

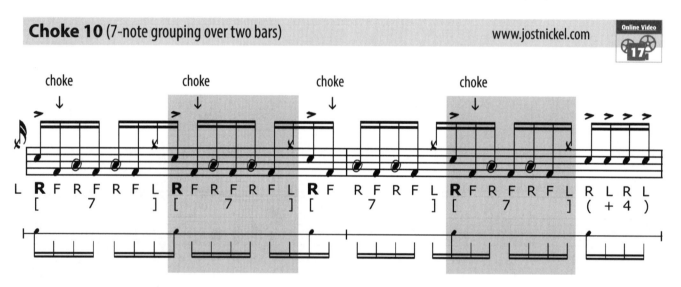

Finally, here is a combination of the *6-, 5-, and 7-note groupings* of this chapter.

Play the 6-note grouping *twice*, the 5-note grouping *twice*, and the 7-note grouping *once* at the end, where the last beat of the 7-note grouping is a flam on the snare drum.

Choke 11 (Combination fill)   www.jostnickel.com

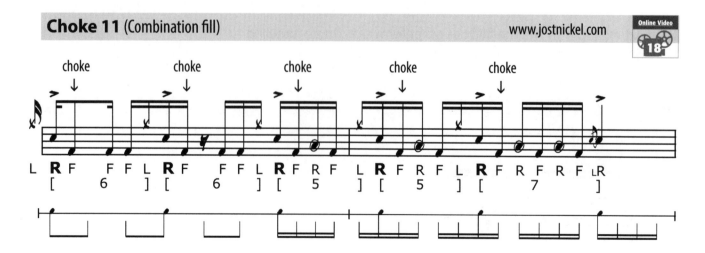

Cymbal Choke plus Hand and Foot Roll

I really like to combine the *hand and foot roll*, which you know from *Chapter 9*, with a choked cymbal. Here is a figure using sixteenth-note triplets.

Play the cymbal with your *right hand*, but choke it with the *left hand* at the same time as the snare beat at the end of the figure (the choke is marked in the notation by an *arrow* from underneath).

Choke 12 (Sixteenth-note triplets | original figure)

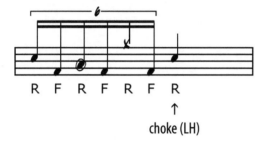

Now play this figure *twice* so the fill lasts for one bar.

Choke 13 (Sixteenth-note triplets | original figure over one bar)

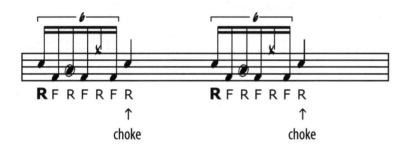

It sounds really good when you start the hand and foot roll on an offbeat—for example, on beat 1+ in the following example.

Choke 14 (Sixteenth-note triplets | original figure displaced by one eighth note)

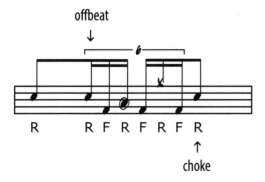

You should combine the start on the downbeat with the start on an offbeat together in a fill. Here is a *one-bar fill* first with the underlying rhythm in *line 2*.

Choke 15 (Sixteenth-note triplets | alternated downbeat and offbeat 1)

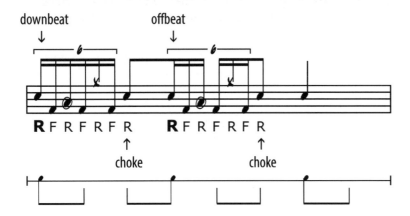

Finally, here is the same idea as a *two-bar fill* with the underlying rhythm in *line 2*.

Choke 16 (Sixteenth-note triplets | alternated downbeat and offbeat 2)   www.jostnickel.com

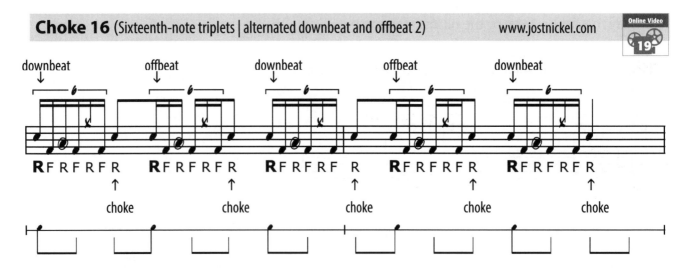

Stick Shot

The characteristic wooden sound of the *stick shot* comes from the fact that you hit one stick against another. With the first hit, you press the stick tip against the head of the drum. In doing so, you apply just enough pressure so the stick doesn't spring back or bounce.

The other hand now hits the stick that is pressed onto the head. Here I'll show you a few of my favorite stick-shot fills, based on rhythmic concepts found in this book.

This note shows the first beat in the notation with the stick tip remaining on the head. This beat will always be played by the *left hand*.

This note shows the following beat in the notation where the *right hand* plays on the stick you hold with your *left*.

Stick Shot 1

This one kicks off with the *4- and 2-note groupings using sixteenth notes*, which you already know from *Chapter 2* (*see page 30*). The stroke played at the beginning of the 4-note grouping stays on the head. Play all beats of the right hand on the stick held in the left hand.

Stick Shot 1 (Original figure)

4-note grouping

L   R   R   F

2-note grouping

R   F

Combine these groupings with **Reading Text 1** (*4- and 2-Note Groupings Using Sixteenth Notes*). *Combination 1* of this reading text is the basis for the following fill.

4		4		4		4		2	4		4		4		2
1	+	2	+	3	+	4	+	1	+	2	+	3	+	4	+

To recap: When combined with the 2-note grouping, the position of the 4-note grouping alternates between the downbeat and the eighth-note offbeat.

Stick Shot 1.1 (Combination 1 from Reading Text 1)   www.jostnickel.com

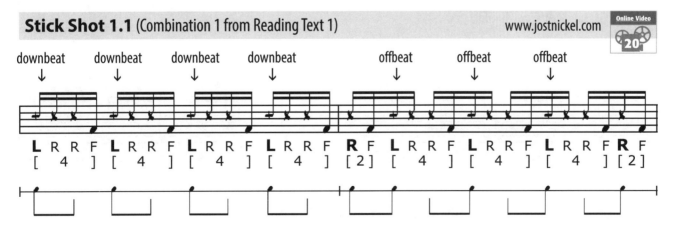

In **Reading Text 1**, you'll find more combinations of 4- and 2-note groupings, which are great for practicing!

Practice Steps	
Start tempo	Quarter note = 70
Number of tempos	3
Number of rounds per tempo	Every fill of the reading text 2 times
Musical form	2-bar groove + 2-bar fill
Count out loud	Quarter note and "click" | sixteenth notes when required
Duration of exercise	Around 15 minutes

Stick Shot 2

Now change the subdivision, and play the 4-note grouping using sixteenth-note triplets.
In *Preliminary Exercise 1*, start on beat 1 (*downbeat*), and play the 4-note grouping three times with one double beat on the bass drum to finish.

Stick Shot 2.1 (Preliminary Exercise 1 | downbeat)

In *Preliminary Exercise 2,* play the exact same figure displaced by one eighth note. The fill starts on beat 1+ (*offbeat*).

Stick Shot 2.2 (Preliminary Exercise 2 | offbeat)

Combine both preliminary exercises in a *two-bar fill*. The figure will change between the downbeat and the offbeat.

Stick Shot 2.3 (Two-bar fill)   CD 58

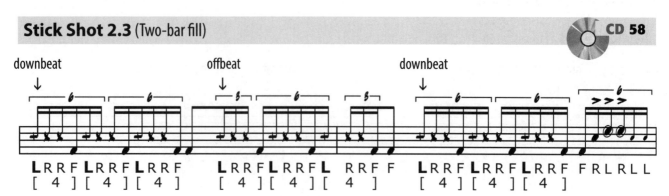

You can play the end of the fill however you'd like (in bar 2 on beat 4).

Stick Shot 3

We now come to a stick-shot fill based on the *3-, 5-, and 7-note grouping using sixteenth notes*. All groupings start with the left hand. All beats of the right hand will be played on the stick of the left hand.

Stick Shot 3 (Original figure)

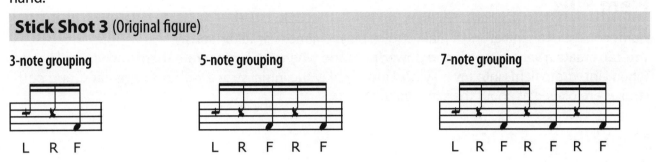

Combine these three groups with **Reading Text 9** (*3-, 5-, and 7-Note Grouping Using Sixteenth Notes II*). *Combination 1* of this reading text is the basis for the following fill.

3	**3**	**5**		**5**		**7**		**7**		**+2**
1 e + a	2 e + a	3 e + a	4 e + a	1 e + a	2 e + a	3 e + a	4 e + a			

The underlying rhythm is in *line 2*.

Stick Shot 3.1 (Combination 1 from Reading Text 9)   **CD 59**

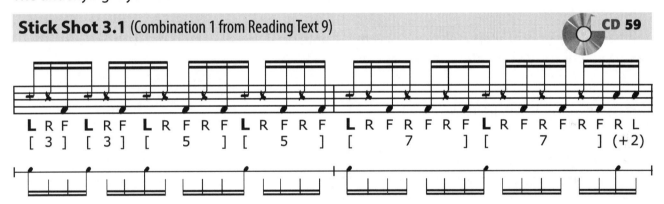

Reading Text 9 shows *nine* different combinations in which to practice the stick shot.

Practice Steps	
Start tempo	Quarter note = 70
Number of tempos	3
Number of rounds per tempo	Every fill of the reading text 2 times
Musical form	2-bar groove + 2-bar fill
Count out loud	Quarter note and "click" | sixteenth notes when required
Duration of exercise	Around 15 minutes

If **Reading Text 9** is too difficult, play **Reading Text 8** (*3-, 5-, and 7-Note Groupings Using Sixteenth Notes I*). It is easier to play because it only combines two of the three groups.

If you like playing the 3-, 5- and 7-note groupings using eighth-note triplets, play **Reading Text 10** (*3-, 5-, and 7-Note Groupings Using Eighth-Note Triplets I*), in which only two of the three groups are combined, and finish with **Reading Text 11** (*3-, 5-, and 7-Note Groupings Using Eighth-Note Triplets II*).

Flam Fills

Flams consist of an initial and a main stroke, played almost simultaneously.
You can create a very compact and powerful sound when you incorporate them into your fills.
When I integrate flams into my playing, I mostly play the initial stroke with the right hand, and both strokes are played at about the same volume.

Flam Fills 1

One of my favorite flam figures is a 3-note grouping using sixteenth notes—you'll get to know it on the snare drum first. Pay attention to the accents!

Flam Fill 1 (Original figure)

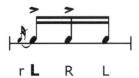

r **L**   R   L

The hands always play alternately! Now play this 3-note grouping over *two bars*. It also sounds good when you only play one of the two bars as a fill.

Flam Fill 1.1 (Original figure over two bars)

r**L** R L r**L** R L r**L** R L r**L** R L r**L** R L r**L** R L r**L** R L r**L** R L r**L** R L r**L** R L R L
[3] [3] [3] [3] [3] [3] [3] [3] [3] [3] (+2)

Now the *orchestration* changes. Play the second beat of the 3-note grouping on the ride cymbal, together with the bass drum.

Flam Fill 1.2 (Original figure with ride cymbal)

r **L**   R   L

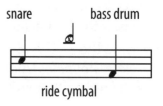

snare   bass drum

ride cymbal

Play this orchestration of the 3-note grouping over *two bars*.

Flam Fill 1.3 (Ride cymbal figure over two bars)

Another small change in the orchestration can be created by playing the initial stroke on the floor tom. The inclusion of the toms is a reason why I play the initial stroke with the right hand: if you split the flam between the snare drum and floor tom, it simply sounds fatter when the tom comes before the snare drum.

Flam Fill 1.4 (Original figure with ride cymbal and floor tom)

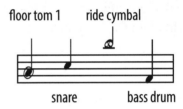

... and now over *two bars*.

Flam Fill 1.5 (Ride cymbal with floor tom over two bars)

CD 60

Practice Tip

Now play the same figure using eighth-note triplets. As the subdivision of your fill has changed, play it in combination with a shuffle groove.

Musical Form

If you play the 3-note grouping using eighth-note triplets, the underlying rhythm is simple (*quarter notes, see line 2*). It seems very easy at first, but it sounds great as a fill.

Flam Fill 1.6 (3-note grouping using eighth-note triplets)

When fills start prominently with an accent on the snare drum, I often play them from beat 2. You get a smooth transition between the groove and fill because the groove also has snare accents on beats 2 and 4. If your fill starts with an accent on beat 1, it's quite fractured (which isn't necessarily a bad thing). In *Flam Fill 1.7,* you'll see three bars of groove followed by *Flam Fill 1.6*, but now starting on beat 2.

Flam Fill 1.7 (3-note grouping using eighth-note triplets starting on beat 2) **CD 61**

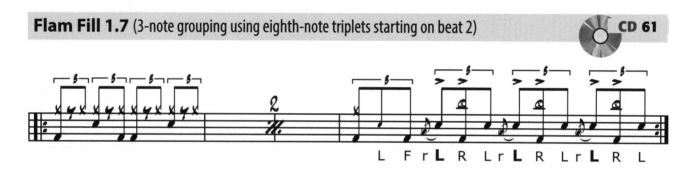

The other two positions of the 3-note grouping in a shuffle are also interesting. First, play the flam on the *third beat* of the eighth-note triplet. I start this fill with the flam as a prelude on the last beat of the previous bar.

Flam Fill 1.8 (3-note grouping using eighth-note triplets | Position 2) **CD 62**

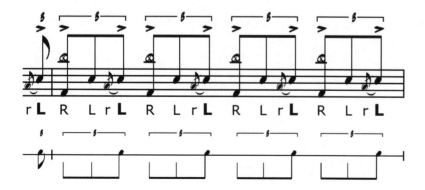

Now we come to the last position, where the flam is played on the *second beat* of the eighth-note triplet. This comes last because I feel it is more rhythmically challenging as a starting point than the other two.

Flam Fill 1.9 (3-note grouping using eighth-note triplets | Position 3)

CD 63

L r **L** R   L r **L** R   L r **L** R   L r **L** R

Flam Fills 2 (Blushda)

The next flam fill is called a *blushda* and is derived from the first flam fill of this chapter (*Flam Fill 1*). *Flam Fill 1* is in *line 1* and the *blushda fill* in *line 2*. There are two small changes:

1. The stroke on the second sixteenth note is doubled, so instead of playing a sixteenth note, play *two 32nd notes* with the *right hand*.

2. Emphasize both strokes that are played with the *left*.

Flam Fill 2 (Original figure)

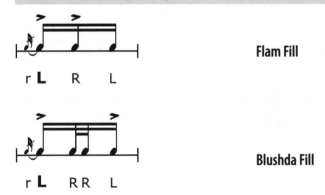

Flam Fill

r **L**   R   L

Blushda Fill

r **L**   R R   L

The *left hand* is very important in playing the blushda. Here is a preliminary exercise where you only play the *left hand* in *bar 1* and then the *entire* fill in *bar 2* (up to beat 4). The left hand plays exactly the same thing in *lines 1* and *2*!

Flam Fill 2.1 (Preliminary Exercise 1)

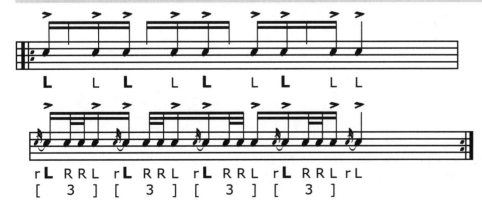

L   **L**   **L**   **L**   **L**   **L**   **L**   **L**   **L** **L**

r **L** R R L   r **L** R R L   r **L** R R L   r **L** R R L r **L**
[3   ]   [3   ]   [3   ]   [3   ]

Extend this preliminary exercise to *two bars*. Only play the *left hand* in *bars 1 and 2,* and the blushda in *bars 3 and 4*. Again, the *left hand* plays exactly the same thing in *lines 1* and *2*.

Flam Fill 2.2 (Preliminary Exercise 2)

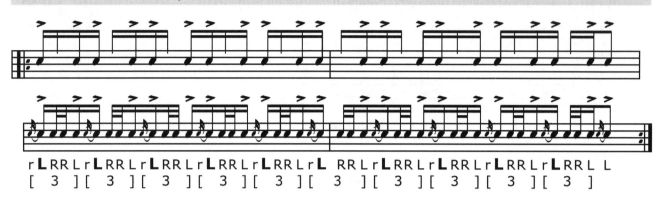

```
r L RR L r L RR L r L RR L r L RR L r L RR L r L   RR L r L RR L r L RR L r L RR L r L RR L L
[  3  ][  3  ][  3  ][  3  ][  3  ][  3  ][  3  ][  3  ][  3  ][  3  ]
```

When you have mastered the blushda, you can try the following two orchestrations. In the first orchestration, play the initial stroke (**RH**) on the *floor tom*. The rest remains unchanged.

Flam Fill 2.3 (Floor tom as initial stroke)

```
r L   RR   L
```

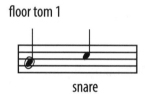

floor tom 1

snare

Flam Fill 2.4 (Floor tom as initial stroke over two bars)

CD 64

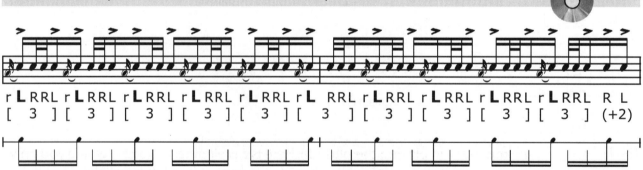

```
r L RR L r L RR L r L RR L r L RR L r L RR L r L   RR L r L RR L r L RR L r L RR L r L RR L  R L
[  3  ][  3  ][  3  ][  3  ][  3  ][  3  ][  3  ][  3  ][  3  ][  3  ] (+2)
```

Another orchestration idea would be to have the right hand play the initial stroke on the ride cymbal, together with the bass drum.

Flam Fill 2.5 (Ride cymbal with BD as initial stroke)

```
r L   RR   L
```

ride cymbal   snare

bass drum

You can also play this orchestration over *two bars*. For a *one-bar fill*, play either the first or second bar. The sticking and underlying rhythm are identical to *Flam Fill 2.4*.

126

Flam Fill 2.6

CD 65

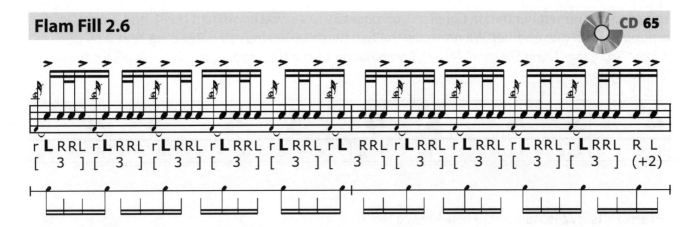

r L RRL r L RRL r L RRL r L RRL r L RRL r L RRL r L RRL r L RRL r L RRL r L RRL R L
[3] [3] [3] [3] [3] [3] [3] [3] [3] [3] (+2)

Flam Fills 3 (Blushda as a 4-Note Grouping)

Let's extend the blushda by one beat to make it a *4-note grouping*. The new fourth beat is another flam. I have chosen the orchestration in which the initial stroke is played on the floor tom, but obviously you can play the initial stroke on the snare drum instead. I suggest practicing the orchestration in which the initial stroke is being played with the ride cymbal (and bass drum) last, as it is more difficult than the other two orchestrations.

Flam Fill 3 (Original figure: 4-note grouping)

r **L** RR L r L

For a *one-bar fill*, play the 4-note grouping four times.

Because the *left hand* is so important, here is a preliminary exercise where you only play the *left hand* in bar 1, and then the *entire* fill in bar 2. The left hand plays exactly the same thing in *lines 1* and *2*.

Flam Fill 3.1 (4-note grouping as a one-bar fill with preliminary exercise)

L   L L **L**   L L **L**   L L **L**   L L

r **L** RR L r L r **L** RR L r L r **L** RR L r L r **L** RR L r L

Now combine the 4-note grouping with the *3-note grouping* you already know.

4-note grouping

r **L** RR L rL

3-note grouping

r **L** RR L

You probably remember that in *Chapter 2*, on *pages 39 to 44*, you combined the 4- and 3-note groupings with one another. We now play the two blushda groups using **Reading Text 2** (*4- and 3-Note Groupings Using Sixteenth Notes*). *Combination 1* from this reading text is the basis for the following fill:

Flam Fills 3.2 (Combination 1 from Reading Text 2)   CD 66

Reading Text 2 shows *seven* further combinations of the 4- and 3-note groupings, which you should practice if you would like to delve further into this topic.

Practice Steps	
Start tempo	Quarter note = 60
Number of tempos	3
Number of rounds per tempo	Every fill of the reading text 2 times
Musical form	2-bar groove + 2-bar fill
Count out loud	Quarter note and "click" | sixteenth notes when required
Duration of exercise	Around 15 minutes

You can use **Reading Text 3** (*4- and 3-Note Groupings Using Eighth-Note Triplets*) if you want to play the two blushda groups using eighth-note triplets.

Flam Fills 4 (3-, 5-, and 7-Note Groupings)

3-, 5-, and 7-note groupings form the rhythmic basis of the next fills.

We'll take *Flam Fill 1.2* on *page 122* as the 3-note grouping. The *5- and 7-note groupings* are derived from the 3-note grouping as follows:

To create the 5-note grouping, extend the 3-note grouping by repeating the second and third strokes. The first three strokes are identical (see **gray markings**).

Flam Fill 4.1 (Original figure: 3- and 5-note groupings)

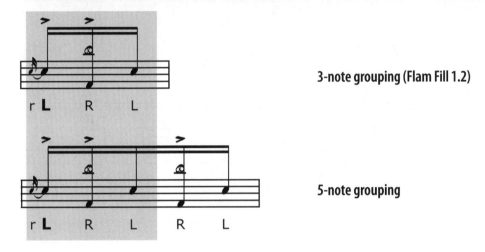

3-note grouping (Flam Fill 1.2)

5-note grouping

To create the 7-note grouping, add the same two strokes on to the 5-note grouping. The first five strokes are identical here (see **gray markings**).

Flam Fills 4.2 (Original figure: 5- and 7-note groupings)

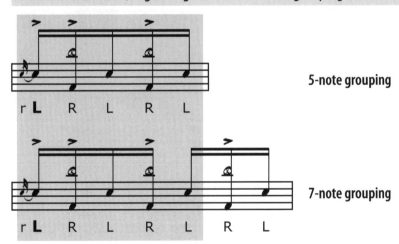

5-note grouping

7-note grouping

Here are the groups described above:

Flam Fills 4.3 (All original figures in an overview)

3-note grouping

5-note grouping

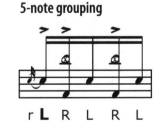

7-note grouping

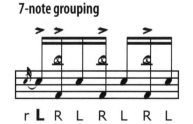

Combine these three groups with **Reading Text 9** (*3-, 5-, and 7-Note Grouping Using Sixteenth Notes II*). *Combination 1* of this reading text is the basis for the following fill.

3	**3**	**5**		**5**		**7**		**7**		**+2**

1	e	+	a	2	e	+	a	3	e	+	a	4	e	+	a	1	e	+	a	2	e	+	a	3	e	+	a	4	e	+	a

The underlying rhythm is in *line 2*.

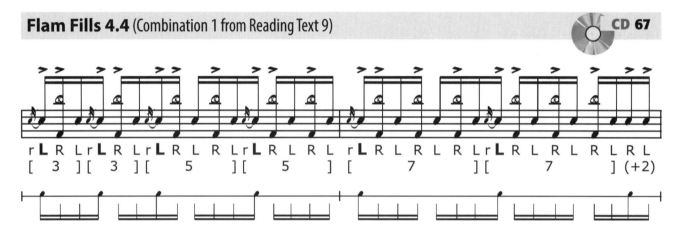

Flam Fills 4.4 (Combination 1 from Reading Text 9)   CD 67

Reading Text 9 shows *nine* different combinations of these flam fills to practice.

Practice Steps	
Start tempo	Quarter note = 70
Number of tempos	3
Number of rounds per tempo	Every fill of the reading text 2 times
Musical form	2-bar groove + 2-bar fill
Count out loud	Quarter note and "click" │ sixteenth notes when required
Duration of exercise	Around 15 minutes

If you find **Reading Text 9** too difficult, start with **Reading Text 8** (*3-, 5-, and 7-Note Groupings Using Sixteenth Notes I*). This is easier to play because it only combines two of the three groups.

If you like playing the 3-, 5-, and 7-note groupings using eighth-note triplets, start with **Reading Text 10** first (*3-, 5-, and 7-Note Groupings Using Eighth-Note Triplets I*), in which only two of the three groups are combined, and then finish with **Reading Text 11** (*3-, 5-, and 7-Note Grouping Using Eighth-Note Triplets II*).

Snare-Drum Exercises with 4- and 2-Note Groupings Using Sixteenth Notes

The *combination of the 4- and 2-note groupings* is a rhythmic concept you can apply in many different ways. The more you're able to master the concept, the easier it will be to transfer it to other motifs. With the following snare-drum exercises, you will further the basic rhythmic idea and also improve your snare-drum technique.

The 4-note groupings for the snare drum look like this:

Snare 1 (Original figure: 4-note grouping)

R R L L

Here's the 2-note grouping (*pay attention to the accents*):

Snare 2 (Original figure: 2-note grouping)

R L

Combine these two groups to make *two-bar fills*. To clarify, here are two examples.

In *Snare-Drum Exercise 1*, always play alternating 4- and 2-note groupings. Therefore the 4-note grouping always changes between the downbeat and the offbeat.

Snare-Drum Exercise 1

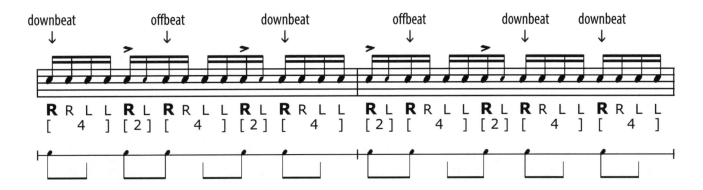

In *Snare-Drum Exercise 2*, play alternating 4- and 2-note groupings, but this time start with the 2-note grouping.

Snare-Drum Exercise 2

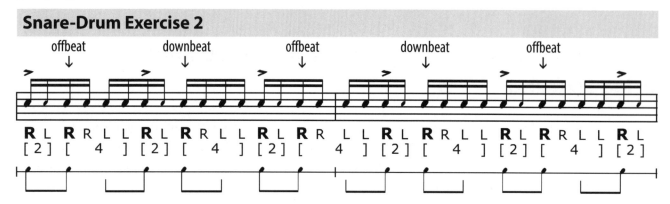

Obviously you should practice more than just the combinations above. For that, take **Reading Text 1** (*4- and 2-Note Groupings Using Sixteenth Notes*) with *nine* two-bar combinations of 4- and 2-note groupings.

Practice Steps	
Start tempo	Quarter note = 70
Number of tempos	3
Number of rounds per tempo	Every fill of the reading text 2 times
Count out loud	Quarter note and "click" | sixteenth notes when required
Duration of exercise	Around 15 minutes

Snare-Drum Exercises with 4- and 3-Note Groupings Using 16th Notes

Combining 4- and 3-note groupings is also a rhythmic concept that can be used universally. With the following snare-drum exercise, you will internalize the basic rhythmic idea. For the 4-note grouping, play **R L L R**, with an accent on the first beat.

Snare 1 (Original figure: 4-note grouping)

For the 3-note grouping, play **R L L**, with an accent in the right hand.

Snare 2 (Original figure: 3-note grouping)

Now combine these groups. To clarify, please see the three examples below. *Snare-Drum Exercise 1* is a four-bar exercise where every position of the 4-note grouping will be played. The 3-note groupings are marked in **gray**.

Snare-Drum Exercise 1

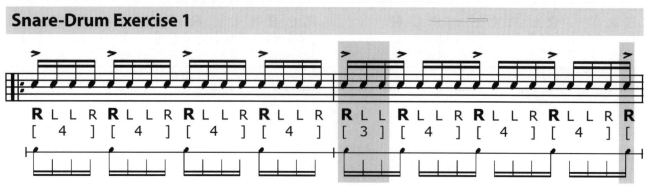

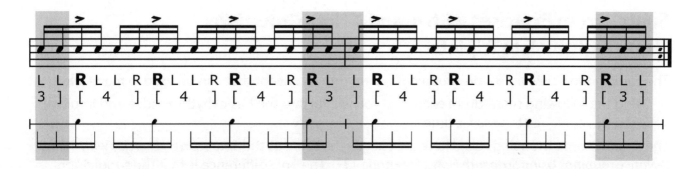

In *Snare-Drum Exercise 2*, play alternating 4- and 3-note groupings starting with the 4-note grouping.

Snare-Drum Exercise 2

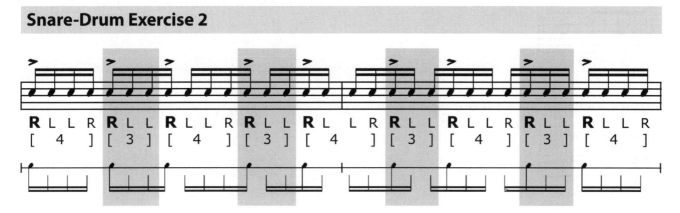

In *Snare-Drum Exercise 3*, you will again play alternating 4- and 3-note groupings, but you'll start with the 3-note grouping.

Snare-Drum Exercise 3

Reading Text 2 (*4- and 3-Note Groupings Using Sixteenth Notes*) shows *eight* different two-bar combinations of the 4- and 3-note groupings you should take as the rhythmic basis for further snare-drum exercises.

Practice Steps	
Start tempo	Quarter note = 70
Number of tempos	3
Number of rounds per tempo	Every fill of the reading text 2 times
Count out loud	Quarter note and "click" | sixteenth notes when required
Duration of exercise	Around 15 minutes

Snare-Drum Exercises with 4- and 3-Note Groupings Using Eighth-Note Triplets

The *combination of 4- and 3-note groupings* is a rhythmic concept that can be used in many ways.

By using the following snare-drum exercises, you will further the basic rhythmic idea and improve your snare technique at the same time.

The 4- and 3-note groupings used here are exactly the same as the *Snare-Drum Exercise with 4- and 3-Note Groupings Using Sixteenth Notes* (*see page 132*). The only difference is that the subdivision changes from sixteenth notes to eighth-note triplets.

Snare 1 (Original figure: 4-note grouping)

Snare 2 (Original figure: 3-note grouping)

Now let's combine these groups. To clarify, here are three examples.
Snare-Drum Exercise 1 is a three-bar exercise in which all positions of the 3-note grouping will be played. The 4-note groupings are marked in **gray**. You can see the basic rhythmic structure in *line 2*.

Snare-Drum Exercise 1

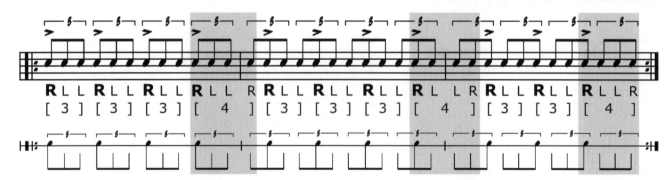

In *Snare-Drum Exercise 2*, play alternating 4- and 3-note groupings, starting with the 4-note grouping.

Snare-Drum Exercise 2

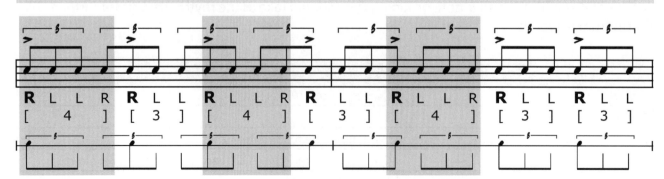

In *Snare-Drum Exercise 3*, play alternating 4- and 3-note groupings again, but this time start with the 3-note grouping.

Snare-Drum Exercise 3

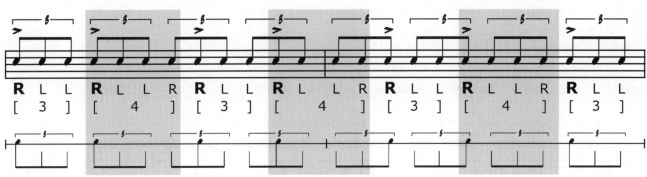

Obviously you should practice more than just the combinations above for these snare-drum exercises. For that, use **Reading Text 3** (*4- and 3-Note Groupings Using Eighth-Note Triplets*).

Practice Steps	
Start tempo	Quarter note = 91
Number of tempos	4
Number of rounds per tempo	Every fill of the reading text 2 times
Count out loud	Quarter note and "click" | eighth-note triplets when required
Duration of exercise	Around 15 minutes

Snare-Drum Exercises with 6- and 3-Note Groupings Using Sixteenth-Note Triplets

You guessed it. *Combining 6- and 3-note groupings* is also a rhythmic concept that can be used in many ways. To further the basic rhythmic idea, we now carry the principle over to a snare-drum exercise.

The 6-note grouping for the snare drum is a *paradiddle-diddle* with an accent on the first beat.

Snare 1 (Original figure: 6-note grouping)

The 3-note grouping below also has an accent on the first beat.

Snare 2 (Original figure: 3-note grouping)

Combine these groups to make *two-bar fills*. To clarify, here are two examples.

In *Snare-Drum Exercise 1*, only play the 6-note grouping in bar 1. In bar 2, play the 3-note grouping once at the beginning, and the 6-note grouping changes to the offbeat after that.

Snare-Drum Exercise 1

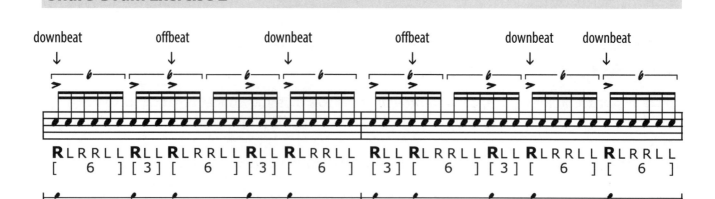

In *Snare-Drum Exercise 2*, always play alternating 6- and 3-note groupings. Therefore, the 6-note grouping always changes between the downbeat and the offbeat.

Snare-Drum Exercise 2

In **Reading Text 4** (*6- and 3-Note Groupings Using Sixteenth-Note Triplets*), you'll find *nine* different two-bar combinations of 6- and 3-note groupings, which can (and should) be used to practice the snare-drum exercises written above.

Practice Steps	
Start tempo	Quarter note = 60
Number of tempos	3
Number of rounds per tempo	Every fill of the reading text 2 times
Count out loud	Quarter note and "click" | eighth notes when required
Duration of exercise	Around 15 minutes

Snare-Drum Exercises with 6- and 4-Note Groupings Using Sixteenth-Note Triplets

Naturally, you can also use the rhythmic concept of *combining 6- and 4-note groupings* in an endless number of ways. You'll have to master it well in order to transfer it to other motifs. Therefore, the following snare-drum exercise aims to make the concept understood as quickly as possible.

The 6-note grouping for the snare drum is a *paradiddle-diddle* and it looks like this:

Snare 1 (Original figure: 6-note grouping)

Here is the 4-note grouping:

Snare 2 (Original figure: 4-note grouping)

Combine these groups to make *two-bar fill*s. To clarify, here are two examples. Even though these exercises are played using sixteenth-note triplets, the underlying rhythm is *eighth-note triplets*. To hear these snare-drum exercises properly, you need to count them as eighth-note triplets. In *Snare-Drum Exercise 1*, mix the 6- and 4-note groupings. The 4-note grouping is marked in **gray**.

Snare-Drum Exercise 1

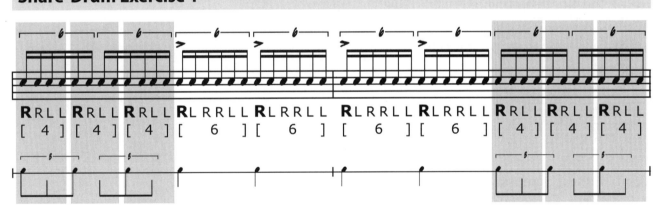

In *Snare-Drum Exercise 2*, play alternating 6- and 4-note groupings, starting with the 4-note grouping.

Snare-Drum Exercise 2

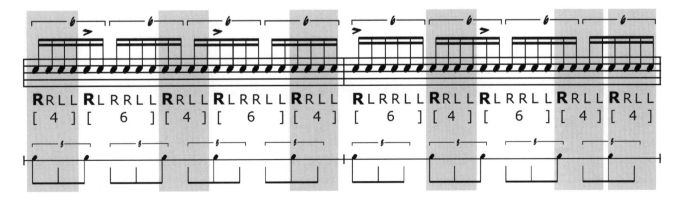

You should also practice more than just the combinations written on the previous page for these snare-drum exercises. For this, use **Reading Text 5** (*6- and 4-Note Groupings Using Sixteenth-Note Triplets*). There you will find *eight* different two-bar combinations of 6- and 4-note groupings.

Practice Steps	
Start tempo	Quarter note = 60
Number of tempos	3
Number of rounds per tempo	Every fill of the reading text 2 times
Count out loud	Quarter note and "click" | eighth-note triplets when required
Duration of exercise	Around 15 minutes

Snare Drum-Exercises with 8- and 4-Note Groupings Using 32nd Notes

Combining 8- and 4-note groupings also lends itself to becoming a snare-drum exercise. You improve your snare-drum technique, further the underlying idea, and make the concept easier to transfer to other motifs. The 8-note grouping for the snare drum looks like this:

Snare 1 (Original figure: 8-note grouping)

R L R L R R L L

Here is the 4-note grouping:

Snare 2 (Original figure: 4-note grouping)

R L L R

Combine these groups to make *two-bar fills*. To clarify, here are two examples.
In *Snare-Drum Exercise 1*, only play 8-note groupings in bar 1. In bar 2, play the 4-note grouping once at the beginning, which means that the 8-note grouping changes to the offbeat after that.

Snare-Drum Exercise 1

downbeat   downbeat   downbeat   downbeat   offbeat   offbeat   offbeat

RLR LRRLL**R**LR LRRLL**R**LR LRRLL**R**LR LRRLL **R**LLR**R**LR LRRLL**R**LR LRRLL**R**LR LRRLL**R**LLR
[8   ][8   ][8   ][8   ] [4][8   ][8   ][8   ][4]

In *Snare-Drum Exercise 2*, play alternating 8- and 4-note groupings. Therefore the 8-note grouping always changes between the downbeat and the offbeat.

Snare-Drum Exercise 2

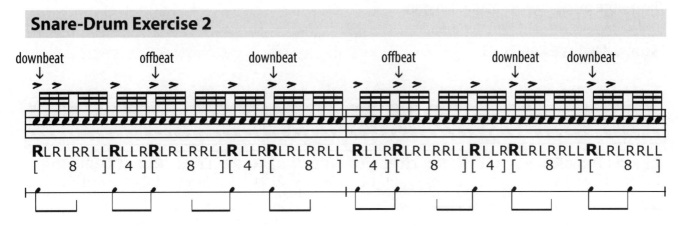

Along with these snare-drum exercises, you should also practice more than just the combinations written above. For this, use **Reading Text 6** (*8- and 4-Note Groupings Using 32nd Notes*). Here you will find *nine* different two-bar combinations of 8- and 4-note groupings.

Practice Steps	
Start tempo	Eighth note = 100
Number of tempos	3
Number of rounds per tempo	Every fill of the reading text 2 times
Count out loud	Quarter note and "click" | eighth notes when required
Duration of exercise	Around 15 minutes

Snare-Drum Exercises with 6-and 4-Note Groupings Using 32nd Notes

To further the basic rhythmic idea of *6- and 4-note groupings using 32nd notes*, we'll now carry the principle over to a snare-drum exercise. The *6- and 4-Note Groupings Using 32nd Notes* used here are exactly the same as the *Snare-Drum Exercise with 6- and 4-Note Groupings Using Sixteenth-Note Triplets* (*see page 137*). The only difference is that the subdivision of fills changes from sixteenth-note triplets to 32nd notes.

The 6-note grouping for the snare drum is a *paradiddle-diddle*, and it looks like this:

Snare 1 (Original figure: 6-note grouping)

Here is the 4-note grouping:

Snare 2 (Original figure: 4-note grouping)

Combine these groups in order to make *two-bar fills*. To clarify, here are two examples.
In *Snare-Drum Exercise 1*, always play alternating 6- and 4-note groupings.
The 4-note groupings are marked in **gray**.

Snare-Drum Exercise 1

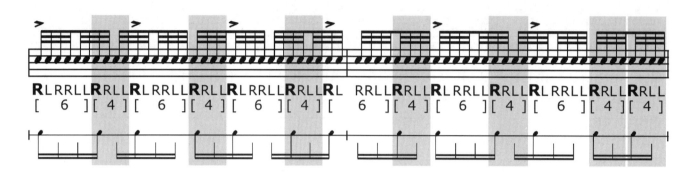

In *Snare-Drum Exercise 2*, play alternating 6- and 4-note groupings again, but start with the 4-note grouping.

Snare-Drum Exercise 2

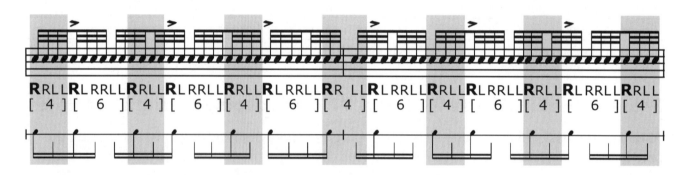

For further practice, use **Reading Text 7** (*6- and 4-Note Groupings Using 32nd Notes*).
Here you will find *eight* different two-bar combinations of 6- and 4-note groupings, which serve as a rhythmic basis for further snare-drum exercises.

Practice Steps	
Start tempo	Eighth note = 100
Number of tempos	3
Number of rounds per tempo	Every fill of the reading text 2 times
Count out loud	Quarter note and "click" | sixteenth notes when required
Duration of exercise	Around 15 minutes

Photo © Drumeo

Photo © Ingo Baron

Photo © Mareike Nickel